Janet Ruckert, Ed.D.

The
Four-Footed
Therapist

HOW YOUR PET CAN HELP
YOU SOLVE YOUR PROBLEMS

TEN SPEED PRESS

This book is available at quantity discount for educational, business, or sales promotional use. Please contact Ten Speed Press for special discount schedules.

P.O. Box 7123, Berkeley, CA 94707

800-841-BOOK   In California: 415-845-8414

1☉
TEN SPEED PRESS
P. O. Box 7123
Berkeley, California 94707

Book Design by Nancy Austin
Cover Design by Brenton Beck

Illustrations by Dina Redman
Composition by Skillful Means Press

Library of Congress Cataloging in Publication Data
        Ruckert, Janet, 1926–
            The four-footed therapist.
            1. Pets – Therapeutic use. 2. Psychotherapy.
I. Title.
RC489.P47R83 1987   616.89'14   86-23123

Printed in the United States of America

1 2 3 4 5 – 90 89 88 87

THE FOUR-FOOTED THERAPIST

To Ouzo
a very special
four-footed Therapist
Janet Ruckert
6/88

CONTENTS

ACKNOWLEDGMENTS

T his book would not be complete unless I acknowledge the support and help I received from my two-legged and four-legged friends. Invaluable encouragement was offered by Irene Webb and Mel Berger. My special thanks and appreciation go to Norman Lobsenz, Victoria Pasternack (and her two cats), Robert Windeler, Janna Wong Healy, and Ron Baron of Norman Winter and Associates. I would also like to thank the staff of the Santa Barbara Writer's Conference for their confidence in this project. Gratitude also goes to my editor, Patti Breitman, and to the staff at Ten Speed Press.

I would also like to thank my patients, who helped with my studies by agreeing to include my four-footed therapists in their therapy. I would like to acknowledge the members of the West Los Angeles Obedience Club, whose patience led to Delilah's receiving a Companion dog degree. In addition, thanks go to the members of the Golden State Rottweiler Club for enhancing my pleasure in, and respect for, rottweilers.

I'd like to acknowledge Leo Bustad, Linda Hines, and the Delta Society for devoting such time and energy to improving the animal–human bond. And thanks are also extended to Hugh Tebault, the Latham Foundation, and Phil Arkow for their knowledge and help.

A special thanks goes to my husband, David, who, with patience and love, helped me train our dogs and bring up our cats, and who volunteered to walk Lorelei and Delilah on those many long weekends while I was busy writing this book.

Finally, I must mention my own pet therapists, Lorelei, Delilah, Clancy, Casey, and Merlin, whose patience and kindness with humans inspired this book and who continually gave their love and support while I wrote it.

Jan Ruckert
Los Angeles, California
May 1987

PREFACE

I f I had read *The Four-Footed Therapist* years ago I might not have
committed two egregious errors of judgement with my daughter
and two different pets . . .

She was 12, I was recently separated, and her brother had
been given a new puppy. Later, Lisa wanted a kitten. I agreed, "on
condition." The combination of kitten and puppy were too much
for me. Without considering the consequence on her self-esteem,
I explained in my most adult manner that we couldn't keep it.

Several years later she was allowed to get a puppy of her own.
Two years later, I decreed that she was not spending sufficient time
with the dog to diffuse its rambunctious manners. After repeated
warnings, again, with my adult reasoning, I gave the dog to someone who lived in the country.

As a grown woman my daughter has struggled with the usual
self-doubts as to her ability to run her own life successfully. I can
see now that my actions were a denial of her autonomy and her
ability to make good decisions.

I do not say my actions were the cause of these self-doubts,
but I can see from the practical suggestions in this book that there
were more creative responses to the situation that would have
recognized the healing power of a pet's unconditional love and
acceptance.

What a wonderful gift to every pet owner, to open our eyes to the love that is right there for us twenty-four hours a day, and how to derive the help we need from it.

Jean Schulz
President, Board of Directors,
Canine Companions for Independence

Producer, "What a Difference A Dog Makes," documentary

INTRODUCTION

Discovering Animal Therapists

I first discovered that animals are natural therapists the day that Clancy, my Burmese cat, came with me to my office. I had been working for several months with an eight-year-old girl who was suffering from a depression brought on by her parents' divorce two years earlier. Cathy* lived with her mother. She had described to me feelings of loneliness and isolation, but had not specifically related these feelings to her father's absence. In fact, Cathy was not able to express any feelings about him at all. I was concerned that the trauma Cathy felt over losing her father might take a long time to surface. But during this visit she laid eyes on Clancy, and she smiled for the first time in four months of treatment.

Cathy sat on the floor, placed the cat in her lap, and stroked his head, while I explained that he was in the office because I was taking him to the vet as soon as our session was over. Clancy returned Cathy's attention by settling into her lap and emitting a loud purr. After a few moments and while still cuddling the cat, Cathy began to tell Clancy how much she missed her father, and how he had played with her, read her stories, and tucked her into bed every night. The tears began to roll down her cheeks.

All names have been changed.

1

Holding and stroking the soft, warm animal had put her in touch with her deep feelings and brought to the surface the painful experience of losing her father's daily attention as well as her sense of a stable family. Because Clancy's appearance helped Cathy break through to these suppressed feelings, he also, in essence, helped her begin to resolve them. Cathy now was ready to begin her journey toward a happy, normal childhood.

The Four-Footed Therapist offers advice on how everyone — children, singles, couples, older people — can use pets to help deal with everyday emotional problems. My version of "petcology" is based on the principles I have developed from using pets as therapists. This book presents those principles. It draws upon hundreds of case histories from my private practice in which pets helped my patients progress in their therapy. Anecdotes and interviews are offered so that you may use the same techniques to understand your problems. An array of exercises and suggestions helps you work out solutions.

One out of every two households in this country already includes an animal. The Four-Footed Therapist teaches you how to use your animal as a counselor. The examples and exercises help you gain insight into, and find solutions for, problems associated with loneliness, lack of self-confidence, passivity, job stress, difficulty committing to a relationship, marital conflicts, midlife changes, child-rearing by single or divorced parents, sibling rivalry, discipline, lack of parent – child communication, and teenage rebellion. It presents suggestions on instigating play and exercise sessions, which in turn improve physical health and lessen psychological stress.

It is important to realize that neither a human nor an animal therapist can *cure* a problem. But either one can act as a catalyst to bring to the surface a person's own natural skills for psychological problem-solving. As I describe the cases in which my pets helped my clients, I alter these self-help exercises for use at home. Although they are not designed to cure difficult problems, such as phobias, severe anxiety, severe depression, substance abuse, or character disorders (the help of a therapist would be essential for that), they do show you how you can use your pet at home to help you cope with less serious psychological problems. In other words, The Four-Footed Therapist doesn't in itself solve your problem, but it serves as a guide to help you find — and put to constructive use — your own healthy, creative abilities for achieving personal growth.

Role playing, fantasizing, and self-affirmations, when used properly, can serve as an impetus for self-growth. Many of the exercises described in this book have been adapted for use with pets from those used by therapists in clinical practice and workshops for years. They do not require the presence of a pet in order to work, but it is not always easy to sit down alone, look at what you are doing in your life, and make constructive changes. With a familiar pet by your side, you'll receive love and support; this is how your pet's presence will help you during the exercises. Your pet's warmth encourages reflection and honesty. At just that moment you may feel something new about yourself and begin to take positive steps toward change.

After the episode with Cathy and Clancy, I decided to bring my dog Lorelei, a German Rottweiler, to the office. Lorelei somehow knew that it was her "job" to give attention, as needed, to the people who sought my help. For example, if someone was sad, she would sit at his or her feet. She would put her head in a patient's lap if she felt the need was there. I noticed how Lorelei helped in therapy with one couple in particular who had been coming to me for several months for help with a marital conflict. Lorelei moved back and forth between them, offering her affection to both. As she sat by the wife's side, the woman felt secure enough to turn to her husband and begin to tell him how much she needed him. I listened from a quiet corner as her voice softened, and she described the early years of their marriage, when she had experienced the same unconditional love from him that Lorelei was giving to her now. When Lorelei sat at the husband's feet, he felt comfortable enough to reveal to his wife that he had felt left out since her return to graduate school, because increasingly she had less time for him. Because he felt rejected he had withdrawn from her. Both were lonely and unable to express their needs to each other. But with the presence of Lorelei, whose company created warmth and security, the two were able to bring their feelings into the open.

As I observed more closely the interaction between pet and person, I could see that in many cases, the animal unconsciously held the key to the human's inner self. I noticed that my pets, for instance, could move through my clients' layers of masks and defenses and easily tap into painful or joyous memories. The animal's presence brought into focus, in a totally instinctive way, what each person felt and needed for his or her emotional well-being. In most cases the animal's attention gave my patients confidence and support enough to allow them to begin deeper exploration into the inner self or an intimate relationship.

When people learn about my work with animals in therapy, they often ask if I use pets with every client. The answer is no. Not everyone who comes to therapy is interested in talking to, or performing psychological exercises with, animals. But most of my clients look forward to seeing one of my dogs or cats in the office, and notice when they are not there. The pets give the office a homey feeling; they encourage the natural relationship that comes from a sense of family. My patients who have pets enjoy doing their psychological homework with their own animals. And I have found that clients with pet therapists progress faster.

Another question I am often asked is How can I practice the exercises if I am allergic to dogs or cats? Other pets, such as birds or fish, have been shown to have the same beneficial effects on blood pressure and longevity as the more conventional pets. Research done in England studied the effects of pet parakeets on the elderly. The study showed that owning a bird caused a significant improvement in self-esteem and increased interest in socializing with others. The elderly subjects stopped talking about their physical problems and started talking about their birds (R. A. Mugford and J. G. M'Comisky, "Some Recent Work on the Psychotherapeutic Value of Caged Birds with Old People," in *Pet Animals and Society*, ed. R. S. Anderson [London: Bailliere Tindall, 1975]). It has been proven that watching tropical fish reduces blood pressure and encourages relaxation (A. H. Katcher, E. Friedmann, A. Beck, and J. Lynch, "Talking, Looking and Blood Pressure: Physiological Consequences of Interaction with the Living Environment," paper presented at the International Conference on the Human-Companion Bond, Philadelphia, October 5–7, 1981).

I have directed this book toward people who are interested in self-growth, but it also gives information and guidance to teachers, nurses, social workers, and psychotherapists who would like to use animals in their work with people. This book, then, is addressed to all those who wish to use the pet–people relationship to enrich lives.

My staff of pet therapists includes three Burmese cats, Clancy, Casey, and Merlin, and two Rottweilers, Lorelei and Delilah. They have given love, attention, and support to many clients who have searched for self-acceptance.

Having an animal at home encourages healthy activity, lowers blood pressure, and offers stable companionship, thus helping us live longer. In the next chapter we will explore in greater depth how animals keep their owners healthy.

CAVEAT

Please note that not all of my patients work with pets during their psychological growth process. I have described those patients who found pet therapy a helpful part of their periods of change. It must also be emphasized that pet therapy is only a part of the patient's interpersonal struggle, which sometimes takes place over a period of many years. I have chosen to report only a portion of the therapeutic process, which in many cases covered years of psychotherapy. The patients that worked best with pets oftentimes had had rewarding childhood experiences with animals, so as adults they were open to the process of working with them in therapy. The incidents I describe highlight moments of contact between pet and patient. Although it may appear to be an easy breakthrough, these therapeutic moments were part of a long process, which necessitated a continuing relationship between patient, therapist, and pet.

Please also note that a number of the cases I describe I learned about through interviews with pet owners or parents of pet owners who were not in therapy. These pet owners had learned to use their pets as emotional allies and supportive models for health. These experiences show how anyone, even if not in therapy, can be helped by a pet therapist.

CHAPTER ONE

Animals Can
Keep You Healthy

PETS AND MENTAL WELL-BEING

A nimals are natural therapists. By their physical presence, responsiveness to human contact, and simple needs, they give their owners a sense of emotional security that is often missing from today's fast-paced and rapidly changing world. Pets offer a consistent, readily available source of warmth, trust, and unconditional love. If we were lucky our mothers were a source of these qualities during our infancy. But, more than likely, we haven't felt them since. Animals, however, with their instinctively loving and attentive qualities, remind us of this blissful state. That early experience of love and protection can be reenacted in our relationships with our animals. Research reports (some of which are mentioned in this chapter) show that animals offer us the benefits of feeling needed, a sense of family, feeling secure, encouragement to exercise, and sensitivity to our moods, among others. Our pets allow us to strip away layers of well-constructed defenses and, in some cases, help us confront our innermost needs.

Extensive surveys compiled by British veterinarian Bruce Fogle in his book *Pets and Their People* (Middlesex, England: Penguin Books, 1983; New York: Penguin Books, 1984), show that pet owners consider their pets to be members of the family. They confide in their pets and believe their pets are sensitive to their moods.

Pets are always loving, available, and completely uncritical. Your pets believe that as their master, you are the most wonderful person in the world. It is not surprising that we relax as we talk to and pet them.

Aaron Katcher, M. D., and Alan Beck, Sc.D., the former a professor of psychiatry and the latter a professor of animal ecology, both at the University of Pennsylvania, examine the meaning of animal companionship in their book *Between Pets and People* (New York: G. P. Putnam's Sons, 1983). Their ongoing research began in 1977 and is conducted at the Center on the Interactions of Animals and Society at the University of Pennsylvania, of which Dr. Beck is head. Their studies support the theory that pet owners indeed humanize their pets. They further relate that this humanization affects one's sense of self-esteem and health.

Treating your pet like a person may sound foolish at first, but most pet owners do it every day. Consider the following "humanization" of family pets:

We name them.

We speak to them.

We feed them our own food.

We sleep with them in our beds.

We take them to the doctors when they're sick.

We make excuses to others for their misbehavior.

We treat them like children.

We bury them and mourn for them when they die.

In a study of 120 pet owners at the veterinary school at the University of Pennsylvania, as reported by Aaron Katcher, M.D., in *Interrelations Between People and Pets* (Springfield, Ill.: Charles C. Thomas, 1981), 98 percent of the people spent time talking to their animals. Interestingly enough, 94 percent said they talked to their pet "as a person," not as an animal. And 81 percent of the owners believed their pets were sensitive to their feelings.

PETS AND PHYSICAL WELL-BEING

In *Between Pets and People,* Drs. Katcher and Beck also stress the importance of the animal-human bond in promoting physical health. They found that the presence of an animal had a beneficial effect on the heart function, and that the intimacy created by talking to and stroking a pet reduced blood pressure and stress. For example, greeting your dog or observing tropical fish in a tank could bring about therapeutic change. They also found that during conversations with others, the mere presence of a pet reduced possible stress during that communication.

Another study at the Center for Interaction of Animals and Society, this one conducted by Erika Friedmann, Ph.D., and included in *Between Pets and People*, studied the relationship between pet ownership and recovery from severe heart disease. She interviewed and recorded information from ninety-two patients hospitalized for coronary disease. Her results showed that the mortality rate among people with pets was one-third that of people without pets. She also found that the therapeutic effect of pet ownership on heart patients was just as strong on married patients as single ones. In the groups studied, the married patients who owned pets did not survive longer than the single ones. The study concluded that pets did not substitute for human relationships, but that they did add to the quality of life and increased patients' chances of survival.

Michael McCulloch, M.D., a psychiatrist in Portland, Oregon, and pioneer in studying the effects of pet ownership on the mentally ill, reports a study in *Interrelations Between People and Pets*. His article, "The Pet as Prosthesis," describes a study of thirty-one patients who were both physically ill and depressed because of the illness and who owned a pet. Using questionnaires, he learned that most patients felt their animals improved morale and gave them a feeling of support during their periods of illness. The respondents reported that their pets distracted them from worry, made them feel more secure, stimulated physical activity, made them laugh, and helped them feel needed. Having a pet depend on them for care helped the patients' self-esteem when they were forced to depend on others. Dr. McCulloch concluded from his study that pet companionship was a support to patient recovery, and that prescription of a pet companion could be appropriate for a number of patients recovering from severe illness.

An animal is a continual source of creativity and surprise. Pet owners are never at a loss for humor and laughter. The antics of unpredictable, energetic pets offer a daily dose of pleasure and fun. This is especially cogent in light of the fact that Norman Cousins, in his books *The Healing Heart* (New York: Avon Books, 1984) and *Anatomy of an Illness* (New York: W. W. Norton, 1979), describes how laughter and pleasure can fight off illness. He tells how the susceptibility to depression relates to physical recovery from heart disease. He also reports on the correlation between a negative state of mind and the possibility of heart disease and cancer.

These are but a few studies investigating the effects of pet ownership on physcial health. They all found that the presence of, and close attachment to, a pet improved morale and physical recovery. Having a pet therapist was not a cure, but it went a long way toward helping patients recover from mental and physical illness. Animals *can* keep us healthy.

TAKING A BREAK
FROM THE FAST TRACK

Deadlines, competition, demanding time commitments, and other job- or school-related stresses take their toll on our minds and bodies. Cardiologists Meyer Friedman and Ray Roseman, in their book *Type A Behavior and Your Heart*, (New York: Knopf, 1974), describe the strong link between personality characteristics and susceptibility to heart attack. They found that those who chronically struggle to achieve more and who are pressured by time constraints are strong candidates for heart disease. These "Type A" personalities are fast-moving people who take on challenging tasks and allow little time to relax. Unrealistic time commitments can shorten one's life.

According to endocrinologist Hans Selye, *The Stress of Life* (rev. ed.) (New York: McGraw-Hill, 1976), the body receives warning signals from the mind and responds with symptoms of chronic stress. These pressures, or stressors, cause the body to react as if it were physically threatened. The result: tense muscles, headaches, stomachaches, sleep disorders, high blood pressure, and increased risk of heart disease. Chronic stress also is cumulative. If we do not tend to it when we first discover it, it will stay with us and haunt our bodies as we grow older, possibly leading to disease.

Besides work or school stresses, there are also personal sources of stress, such as disappointing marital relationships or family conflict. If these feelings of disappointment are not released, they find a place in the body to hide and remind us that something is wrong. Minor frustrations can build and grow until explosions of anger burst forth.

All of us have minor daily problems and frustrations. Stress will not become a habit if we are aware of what causes it, and if we take steps to cope with it. In fact, one of the measures of self-esteem is taking responsibility for our mental and physical health. The campaign to take charge of our health requires time, but it is well worth the effort. Coping with chronic stress is one area in which our pets can offer first aid.

Owning a pet is like living with an instant relaxation therapist. Watching, stroking, playing with, or talking to your pet has an immediately beneficial effect on your body. Just being with a pet reduces blood pressure and lowers anxiety. Notice that your pet finds the most comfortable place in the house to relax; observe his or her stressfree existence. We would do well to learn from this relaxed behavior. A significant number of people who visit a therapist because of tension could benefit from a prescription of pet ownership in order to lower stress.

One candidate for my stress relaxation workshop was Jim. At thirty-six, he was the busiest account executive at his brokerage firm. He typically arrived at the office at 7:00 A.M. to advise customers, all the while scanning the board and the computer. He offered timely recommendations on the market, and consequently his advice was in demand. He enjoyed his work, liked his customers, and felt responsible for them. But the pace of his work was taking its toll on him. Persistent headaches developed. Jim's wife tried to persuade him to take time off, but his pressured pace was too ingrained a habit. When his physician saw that his headaches were caused by his life pattern, Jim was referred to me for treatment. Although Jim came into therapy to cure his headaches, he needed to look at his emotional priorities first.

"I'm on constant alert to the stock market and I'm tied to my phone. My neck tightens up every time I watch the figures come over the tape, because I know what it means to my clients. I feel responsible for their financial losses and gains."

His voice got louder and more tense as he continued to describe his situation. My dog Lorelei, who had been lying on the nearby bean bag chair, sat up and moved to his side. Jim stopped and reached down to pet her. I remained silent because I could see that Jim was content to stroke her head and say nothing. He sank into the couch, and for that instant he felt no demands.

In the months to come, Jim and I looked at his family background and discussed his need for pressure and for responsibility for others. Jim's father had been a bookkeeper who had worked overtime to support his family during the Depression. As the oldest child, Jim had been depended on to care for his younger brothers and sisters while his parents had worked. Both parents had taught Jim a sense of ethical responsibility. His father had frequently talked to him about the state of the country's economy. Jim had grown up with that code and had become a responsible adult, but he had forgotten to take care of his own health. After we had worked on repairing some of Jim's deeply rooted attitudes, I invited him to attend my stress relaxation workshop. I included a number of overworked patients who, like Jim, needed to tone down their stress-inducing activities and learn to relax.

We gathered together on Saturday, in comfortable attire, and made my stressfree animals (the two cats and one of the dogs) our symbols for the afternoon. We sat on the floor and observed them. Lorelei is a large dog, and when she collapses on the floor, she exhibits all the tension of a stretched out pillow! We noticed that the cats lay on the rug and looked bored. We watched their movements. Then we took some deep breaths. We closed our eyes and let the tension move out of our bodies. After a few minutes we were ready to simulate the animals' movements. The participants chose either a dog or a cat as a model. We got down on all fours and crawled. We pawed the rug. We let our imaginations direct our movements. Some of the people growled and jumped about the room in canine fashion. Some others became jungle cats, yowling and moving their bodies in a feline prowl. Everyone got into the animal spirit. The exercises ended in a slow, lazy collapse. The problems and tensions of the human world were far away. This workshop helped the participants integrate into their personal situations what they had learned in therapy.

Exercise One: Animal Relaxation Movement

This is an enjoyable exercise that will help you unwind. You can do it alone, or you can invite a friend to join you. If you don't have a cat or a dog, borrow one. This exercise will help release tension and get you in touch with your body and with animal nature too. It will also make you laugh. The following movements are suggestions that can get you started. From there, use your imagination.

1. Lie down on the rug beside your pet. Close your eyes. Take some deep breaths and feel the tension go out of your body.

2. Open your eyes and look at the posture of your cat or dog. Get on your knees and imitate that posture. If a cat is your model, knead the rug with your fingers, as it does with its claws. Use a pillow and pretend it is your scratching post. Now imagine that you are a cat on the prowl. Move around on the rug in a predatory way. Put your bare feet on the soft rug and feel the "earth" beneath you. Open your mouth and let out a yowl. Stretch out your body. Pretend you are in a jungle.

  If a dog is your model, you can pretend to be a playful puppy. Watch your dog and get ideas for playing and bouncing about. Jump around and imagine you are chasing a ball or a stick. Lie on your back and throw your arms and legs up in the air. Bark.

3. Let yourself enjoy this loose feeling of freedom. This is a chance to laugh and to be silly.

4. Imitate your animal's mood of relaxation by finding the most comfortable place in the room and collapsing.

  When you have finished this exercise, you will have a sense of mental freedom and your body will feel peaceful and relaxed. It's a first step toward learned relaxation, and it comes with the help of your animal therapist.

TRANSFORMING UNWANTED CHANGE INTO GROWTH

The effects of loss and change are not restricted to childhood years. As adults we experience emotional and social "passages." Just because we're adults doesn't mean they are any less frightening. A career change, breakup or marital separation, midlife crisis, or loss of a family member can jolt our equilibrium. These experiences challenge us painfully and sometimes invite ill health. Accepting and learning from these experiences requires courage. Our animals, by reminding us of life's natural cycles, offer a model of hope during these difficult times.

In my practice I have found that the struggle to deal with transitional stress is what often brings people into therapy. During times of loss or change, patients seek solutions. They want to learn how to enrich themselves so that the next step can be a positive one.

Epidemiologist H. G. Wolff, and psychologists Thomas Holmes and Richard Rahe were the first to research the connection between major life changes and illness (T. H. Holmes and H. G. Wolff, "Life Situations, Emotions and Backache," *Psychosomatic Medicine* 14[1952] and R. H. Rahe, "The Pathway Between Subjects: Recent Life Changes and Their Near-Future Illness Reports: Representative Results and Methodological Issues," in *Stressful Life Events: Their Nature and Effects*, ed. B. S. Dohrenwend and B. P. Dohrenwend [New York: Wiley, 1974]). A recent study demonstrates that the way people perceive life changes directly influences their mental and physical health. How you cope with transitions can dramatically affect your health. Those who regard life's movements as negative may develop such symptoms as anxiety, depression, high blood pressure, or even more serious life-threatening diseases. On the other hand, you can learn to transform stress into creative growth, thus keeping your health from deteriorating (J. Johnson and I. Sarason, "Life Stress, Depression and Anxiety: Internal–External Control as a Moderator Variable," *Journal of Psychosomatic Research* 22[1978]).

Adjusting to change and facing the unknown require emotional strength. To achieve that strength you need support from loved ones. A familiar pet during these uneasy periods offers welcome support, possibly even more than family or friends. The companionship of a four-footed pal provides a source of constancy and emotional security, perhaps because our domestic animals maintain an earthy stability. Changes in our home life, friendships, or jobs can cause us to question our self-worth. Our pets love and accept us as we are. They treat us as capable and lovable providers. Their constant appreciation of us helps us deal with these troubled periods.

Barry, one of my clients, went through just such a major life change. He had been the advertising space sales representative for a local magazine for two years and had found himself, at thirty-three, overworked and underappreciated. Each day had been a battle in which he had needed to prove himself. Then the magazine had been sold, he had been fired, and he had dropped into a serious depression. Alone at home his evening bottle of beer had turned into three or four as he had tried unsuccessfully to fight off feelings of rejection. When the depression had continued he had sought help from therapy.

"I don't know why I feel so awful. When I had my job, all I did was complain about it. But since I've been fired, I feel like I flunked out of school. I can't seem to get myself going." Barry fell back onto the pillows of the couch and sat motionless. My dog Delilah went over and gave him a friendly look. He reached down to pet her head.

Barry felt sorry for himself. But brooding at home and indulging in drink were not going to help. We spent many sessions talking about his childhood, how he had ended up at the magazine, and what he wanted to do with his career. He discussed the shame he felt over being fired. During one session I had him perform an exercise with Delilah; he was to talk to her freely, pretending that she could understand how badly he felt. At first Barry had a hard time talking so intimately to the dog. But eventually he described how emotionally isolated he had felt as a child and how much he needed to be accepted. Sitting beside Delilah he let himself reexperience the pain of trying to gain his father's approval. To this end he was in Little League, played quarterback on the high school team, and even entered sports in college. He wanted badly for his father to accept him, and winning in sports was the only way he knew of to bring this about.

"Why couldn't he have loved me for myself? I got so tired pushing myself to the next glory step. I could never stop, not even for a moment," he said as the childhood hurts returned. Barry put his arm around Delilah. It took many sessions, but he had finally allowed himself to feel helpless.

In that moment there were no expectations. He saw how he had created a life trying to please someone else. After talking these feeling out with the help of Delilah, who never passed judgment or expected a certain behavior, he began to experience a sense of freedom. This positive feeling grew in the months to come, and Barry finally took responsibility for his own life.

Later in therapy Barry learned how to accept himself, faults and all. He understood the parts of his personality that he previously had avoided, ones that hadn't fit his father's unrealistic ideal. At my recommendation he adopted a dog. He took good care of her and learned to confide in her. Ginger returned his affection enthusiastically. He took her along on his daily run; this partnered exercise helped him feel better about himself. He also felt it was easier to talk to strangers with Ginger beside him, wagging her tail. He realized he no longer needed his four daily bottles of beer; he could now face his problems.

As Barry learned to accept himself, his own natural interest in his career emerged. By the time he finished therapy, he had started a small publishing company with a friend. His job crisis was the catalyst he needed to reevaluate his direction in life. Then Delilah and Ginger helped him find his healthy self.

Lisa, forty-three, was another patient who suffered because of a major life change. Lisa was a single parent. Divorced at a young age and given custody of her children, she had returned to school right after the divorce and become a legal secretary. She had expected to be proud but somewhat relieved when her youngest child moved away from home fifteen years later. The pride was there, but being forty-three and alone made Lisa anxious. She suffered from an intense feeling of loss. In addition, the sense of abandonment she had felt upon her parents' divorce returned. Soon after, insomnia and headaches began. With her daughters gone Lisa was forced to look at how she had avoided other facets of her life. Her headaches were a sign, as they often are, that something was wrong emotionally.

When Lisa arrived at my office for her first visit, she sank down on the soft pillows of the couch. I waited for her to begin. She looked around the room and talked about the Mexican artifacts and watercolor paintings — anything to delay the pain of describing her latest loss.

"I didn't realize how empty the house would be when Jenny left. I can't believe I complained about the stereo and the late telephone calls. Now it's so quiet. When Jim and I broke up, at least I had the girls. Now I feel so alone."

During the months that followed, Lisa talked about her own parents' divorce. Losing the security of her family created her first feeling of abandonment. Nightmares started and the pattern of insomnia was born.

Because of Lisa's need for company and security, I suggested that she adopt a kitten and practice talking to it about her feelings. The kitten's presence helped Lisa get over her feelings of abandonment. Candide's purr even helped Lisa fall asleep at night. The kitten kept Lisa company while she worked on a collage of pictures that I suggested she put together in order to find some activities that interested her. Looking at the pictures she selected for her collage gave her insight into what she wanted to do next. The following summer, when her daughters came home for a visit, they found a new cat and a more self-assured mother, who would be starting law school in the fall.

Some changes or losses are more difficult to get over, because they require a mourning time. Most common is the death of a spouse; the pain of aloneness can be overwhelming. Often, especially if there were no children, the surviving spouse falls into a depressed pattern, sleeping twelve to fourteen hours every night, afraid to face the long daytime hours. The spouse sometimes feels as if her or his life stopped when the much loved partner died.

The surviving spouse must find her or his own dreams — sometimes dreams that were left behind many years before — and turn these dreams into actuality. Animal therapists can be helpful in the months or years of hard work it takes for the survivor to relearn self-expression. Having a loving, supportive pet is calming for shattered nerves. And if the survivor has a newly adopted dog and takes it through obedience school, she or he will learn how to give firm directions. Being forceful and clear about a dog's training is good practice for learning self-assertion. Eventually, the surviving spouse will learn to put dreams to positive use instead of simply mourning indefinitely.

The initial reaction to loss or change in a familiar and safe life can be potentially dangerous to physical or mental health. But recognizing and then dealing with this stress offfers the opportunity to create new directions in life. The new changes can also bring fear.

Guidelines for Adjusting to Change

Our animals can offer support in this often frightening transition. Learn to use your pet therapist during this time of change. Following is a list of suggestions that can help avert illness in a period of major change.

1. Keep a part of your life familiar in order to offset the shock of change. If you have lost a job or a partner or have undergone some other difficult change, you need a dependable support. Turn to your pet; hug it and talk to it. Your pet can give you a much needed feeling of constancy. Take advantage of this sense of security.

2. Your attitude toward change can affect your potential for illness. Allow yourself to view this change as an opportunity to grow. You can use this time to reflect and to resolve unfinished situations in your life. Talk to your pet and try to express some of the fears that you heretofore have avoided. Use your pet as an accepting friend who listens as you talk.

3. Make a picture of where you are in your life. With your pet friend beside you, make a personal collage, as Lisa did. Sit with your pet and cut out dozens of pictures from magazines that reflect your personality and interests. Then paste them onto a large sheet of cardboard. Don't ponder. Just allow your spontaneity to guide you. When you're done, sit with your pet and reflect upon what you see. Do you have clusters of interests? What do the images say about you? Have you neglected some talents and interests that you could pursue? What is missing from your life? Use this collage to start a plan for yourself.

4. Reach out to new people and new interests; use your pet as an icebreaker in these situations.

5. Exercise. Your dog can be a helpful partner in this venture.

6. If you have a dog, take it to obedience school. You will gain a sense of confidence as you take charge and learn new attitudes.

7. Promise yourself to try a new experience each week, and keep a calendar of each event. If you are raising a young pet, you will have before you a perfect example of daily learning and growth. Observe how change takes place in your animal. There is a youthful part in you that can learn in the same way your pet does.

Following these suggestions and adding more of your own will start you on a creative path that can transform a stressful loss into a productive change.

USING YOUR PET TO ENJOY A LONGER LIFE

No matter how old we actually are, our pets view us as young and healthy. In a society that puts a premium on youth and beauty, our animals show no prejudice. In particular, pets provide a feeling of security and a sense of safety to the senior citizen. Many older people who live alone find that their pets give them a feeling of being needed. This is an important fact to consider, because the need to nurture does not diminish with age. Being physically and socially active with a pet is a good prescription to prevent feeling old.

Lonely older people sometimes paradoxically avoid activities that can be involving and rewarding. But this wasn't the case with Hetti, a transplanted Englishwoman. She was sixty when she became resident director of the local Cat Care Center, thus taking over the mothering of two hundred orphan cats. Many of the center's older volunteers have found that caring for the felines is an involving sidelight; for Hetti, it is a full-time job.

The seeds of her animal love were planted young. At age nine she threatened to jump off a rooftop to prevent her father from drowning an unwanted kitten. That was the first kitten she saved and now, at age seventy-five, she is still fighting the battle on behalf of unwanted cats. "When I was a girl, I thought of becoming a nurse. But when Mother died, I cut short my education and went home to care for three brothers and one sister. My cats were devoted friends during that time of my youth. I love my cats. I admit, I baby them. But mothering comes naturally to me. Today I get up at 4:30 every morning to cook, clean, and nurse our homeless cats. I serve them two meals a day and give formula in bottles to the orphaned kittens too young to eat a regular cat diet."

Her latest challenge is to find a way for cats to live with their owners in local nursing homes. "The elderly should never have to give up their pets. After all, animals are family." Despite all this work, Hetti is full of energy, which she says comes from the love she receives from the cats.

Hetti never married and asserts that she is happier than many of the "married folk" she knows. Her love for animals has given her a full life. Her battle to protect and to find homes for orphan cats gives her a purpose and a place in her community.

Another way that pets can help us live longer is in promoting exercise. Exercise is necessary for people of all ages, but as we get older, it is easier to find reasons to avoid it. Fortunately, our dogs accept no excuse. Dog walking not only adds to our physical well-being, but it is an excellent source of social contact. A daily canine walk provides a chance to talk to neighbors and to meet new people, as it opens conversation possibilities.

All pet owners understand the sense of emotional satisfaction they derive from stroking their animals. But people who live alone receive an especially satisfying sense of intimacy and pleasure from holding and talking to their pets. Tactile needs often increase with age; gently touching and quietly talking to a loving animal can help an elderly person battle the dragon of loneliness.

Warding Off Loneliness

As people grow older, many of the changes that come into their lives are stressful and potentially depressing. Having the constancy of their pet lowers anxiety and offers a sense of emotional security for the future. Although pets are not a substitute for people, they are always there, with their youthful animal spirit.

Aimee, sixty, is a slim, attractive widow whose pets helped her get through a period of sadness and loneliness. Five years ago her only child moved to another state, and soon after her husband died unexpectedly. She found herself suffering badly from loneliness. It was then that a friend suggested she take in a stray cat. The cat's presence eased her pangs of loneliness by offering her steady, loving companionship. Now Aimee takes care of rescued dogs and cats. Her animal family consists of three dogs and three cats — all orphans. "My cats have helped me so much! They bring out my motherly instinct," she told me one day. "I can't pass up a lost cat. They have such a calming influence when they are in the mood to purr. I love the excitement of their unpredictability." Aimee is certain that adopting her dogs has also contributed to her satisfaction and pleasure in life, and helped her get over her loneliness.

Volunteer Work for Animal Organizations Brings Rewards

Organizations that promote animal causes are a ready source of social interest for those seeking involvement opportunities, especially older people. Donating time to these shelters by helping place orphan pets or providing care not only is good for the animals but is an engaging activity with rewarding results. The feeling of being needed is a great antidote to loneliness and inactivity. In addition, having a common interest with other pet lovers helps to create bonds of friendship.

My own love of animals has brought me into numerous pet groups, and I have observed the enthusiasm of older pet lovers firsthand. In interviewing them I was given some highlights of their involvement with their own animals and with the various pet organizations to which they have belonged.

One of these pet lovers is Martha, a kind woman in her sixties. Her first experience with pets was more than fifty-five years ago, when her father brought home three Boston bull terriers. She had developed polio at age six, and she remembers how her dogs stayed beside her on her bed and kept her company. A while later, when one of the dogs got pregnant, giving the puppies care helped Martha recover her health. Coming home from school and talking to her canine friends was an afternoon ritual for her. She still can remember vividly her worry when one of the dogs got lost, and the relief she felt when it was found. Today Martha looks out for lost pets. She is in charge of pet placement for Animal Alliance in Los Angeles, one of the many nonprofit organizations in this country that helps place orphan pets and arranges for medical assistance to needy pets. She and her army of volunteers answer queries of those interested in the organization's services, rescue strays, and offer advice and support. They even take a few of the more well-behaved dogs to local convalescent homes for short visits with its patients.

"Each animal that comes to us is a challenge," Martha said to me. "For instance, we recently obtained a blind Irish setter named Flame. Obviously, we had to be very selective about its new home. Finally, we located a minister's family; they took her in and both parties are happy. I have found over the years that there is always a perfect home for a pet if we have the patience to keep looking. And, as a personal bonus, keeping busy with the animals leaves me no time to worry about myself."

Among the hundreds of successful adoptions, Martha informs me that many are with older people who, after losing a spouse, seek the comfort of a pet. In fact, one of Martha's pet placement assistants is her eighty-six-year-old mother, who likes to cook. It's hard to know who appreciates her gourmet interest more: the orphan animals or her four great-grandchildren! "Mother and I expect to live a long time with our animals. My grandfather kept dogs all his life and he lived to be 104. He worked every day of his adult life."

Another person who has found pleasure from volunteering her time to a worthy animal organization is Laura, sixty-seven. She got her first cat when she started kindergarten, and has owned cats ever since. Laura is a well-known actress, and so she has often offered her name to help publicize local cat events. From there it was a natural step for her to join the board of directors of a cat preservation club and help to organize its annual cat show. Laura's love for cats and her energy are unfailing. Her skills at raising money help support the cats that live at the pet orphanage. When Laura's husband died the friends she met through these activities were there to offer support and company. In addition, her writing skills are enjoyed by the readers of *Paw*, a local cat magazine. Each month she commissions a high school art student to illustrate the newest cat orphans. Laura's keen interest in cats provides her with a healthy link to the younger generation. Besides encouraging their interest in animals, she serves as a role model for other older persons who may be in need of pet companions.

Dog Breeding as a Profession

Dog breeders are special. They are active, caring, and work hard at their jobs, often waking in the wee hours to carry out their responsibilities. On weekends they wash, groom, and exercise their dogs. On Sunday nights they often get together and swap dog-show stories with other breeders. If there is a dog or owner in need, they are always available. They agree that breeding is a tough but rewarding profession.

Mary has been a Rottweiller breeder for twenty years. She imported some of the first Rottweillers from Germany and started a local club to protect the health and quality of the breed. She has kept track of her dogs as they have grown up and competed in shows. Recently, she organized a jogging event for dogs and their owners. The two-legged runners had to strain to keep up, but everyone made it to the finish line! Traveling to dog shows all over the country and caring for her own two dogs keeps Mary and her husband busy and active. They don't have time to brood about getting older. In other words, their dogs are keeping them from aging too quickly.

Obedience Training Can Keep You Healthy

Dorothy and Jim are both seventy-seven and have been married for fifty-three years. Twenty years ago they got involved in dog training by accident. Dorothy adopted a dog from the pound and bought obedience lessons for the dog and Jim as an anniversary present. Dog obedience practice became an engaging hobby. They took their Lhasa Apso up to a utility degree, one of the first for that breed in the United States. As a result of the Lhasa's success, both Dorothy and Jim became active in their local obedience club. Dorothy teaches a weekly problem-solving class, and Jim runs the group practice sessions. In addition, Dorothy and Jim rescue stray dogs. One of the dogs they rescued was an Afghan hound named Jomar. At first they spent many frustrating hours training this animal for obedience work. But their efforts paid off. To their delight he passed the required trials in the ring and received his companion dog degree. (The companion dog degree is the first step of obedience competition, which was set up and is regulated by the American Kennel Club. The dog accumulates points during a trial, and can earn the CD title if successful in three separate novice obedience trials. In each trial the animal must score at least 170 points out of a possible 200. Dogs receive points for such exercises as heeling on and off leash, standing for examination, sitting at attention, and lying at attention. The pet owners whose dogs earn a degree usually exhibit a great deal of patience and dedication.)

Dorothy sat beside me at our obedience club match as I waited my turn to take Delilah into the ring for a practice run. Dorothy explained to me how dogs kept her life busy and happy. "Dogs never complain. They don't get upset about the same things humans do. They are satisfied with three meals a day and loving care. I tell Jomar all my troubles. It's like having another person in the family. Taking our dogs to shows is a great activity for us; we're outdoors all day mingling with other dog owners. We also have parrots. Our latest is Polly, who is sixty-five years old and can speak thirty-five words. Her favorite phrase is 'Let's go,' and that's just what we do! Living with our menagerie of animals gets us out to enjoy life!"

Avoiding the Pitfalls of Pet Ownership

Pet ownership, however, is not all a bed of roses. Pet owners experience problems when they must move and find that they and their charges are not welcome tenants. In this case the animal lover must decide whether to give up a beloved pet or search for an alternative to the dilemma.

Angela was one of my patients, and her love for her cat put her into just such a situation. She had been in therapy for a year while she adjusted to the loss of her husband. Not only did she miss her spouse of many years, but she felt rejected by old friends, who no longer included her in their activities. Angela had to learn how to socialize again. She decided that moving to a larger apartment building would be less costly, and it would also force her to make new friends.

Angela was surprised to find that she and her cat, Winston, were not wanted in many of the apartment buildings that interested her. Her first reaction was to retreat and to feel sorry for herself. But that didn't last long. She took on the battle of the no-pets clause in rental housing. By the time she found a suitable place for the two of them, she had organized a local group to stop animal discrimination in housing. She and her friends started a newsletter, with suggestions on how to bridge the gap between pet owner and landlord. Her group wrote to government officials and caused a stir in local politics. Fighting for fair pet housing was a worthy cause for Angela, and it helped her feel needed again.

Angela's experience with landlords was not unusual; discrimination against pet owners, unfortunately, is common. If you find yourself in a similar circumstance, here are some suggestions to help you through this trying time:

1. If you see an apartment that interests you but it has a "No Pets Allowed" sign, don't give up. Meet the landlord and then describe your pet. Bring a letter of reference from your previous landlord or from former neighbors. Have it state how long you lived in your home and how troublefree the experience was. If you have a dog, describe the advantages of having a canine around for security against burglars or fires. Let your prospective landlord know that you will follow leash laws and clean up after your canine. Bring veterinary records to show your animal's good health.

2. Consider introducing your pet to the landlord. Meeting a lovable and well-behaved pet often can break down the last shred of resistance.

3. The landlord may request an additional security deposit for your pet. If you consider the amount fair, agree to the request. State clearly in writing that any damage done by your pet will be repaired immediately, at your expense.

If none of these suggestions work, there are organizations that offer information to pet owners on finding housing. They also offer pet owners free legal advice. (These organizations are listed in Appendix A.) If you are a pet owner and apartment tenant, you might consider joining one of these organizations and taking an active role to stop housing discrimination against pet owners. Legislation and research are available to support your case. A federal law (passed in 1983) prohibits owners of federally assisted rental housing for the elderly or handicapped from restricting the ownership of pets.

In addition, a study done by Lynette Hart, Ph.D., at the School of Veterinary Medicine at the University of California at Davis show that pets are not likely to create noise problems, personal injury, or property damage. A comprehensive telephone survey was conducted of housing managers of the 113 city and county housing authorities in California (a state where pets have been allowed, since 1982, in the governmentally assisted program). The interviews focused on the drawbacks of introducing pets into housing for the elderly. Besides the telephone survey, the researchers performed on-site interviews with both managers and tenants and found that housing authorities that adopted and enforced clear pet policies, and those that used available community resources that support pet ownership, had few complaints about pets in residence. Dr. Hart's research reported that managers found senior residents to be responsible pet owners who benefited from the companionship of their pets, showed positive changes in mental attitudes, exercised more regularly, and felt more secure. Dr. Hart believes these findings are particularly important, because California was the first state to introduce pets into public housing for the elderly (Lynette A. Hart, "Effects of Pets in California Public Housing for Elderly: Perspectives of Residents and On-Site Managers," paper presented at the Delta Society International Conference, Living Together: People, Animals, and the Environment, Boston, August 20–23, 1986).

So don't give up your efforts to find a home for you and your pet. For young and old, keeping an animal helps to counteract the stress of urban life as well as helps you live longer.

Using Pets to Close Generation Gaps

Pets create personal contact; they can even close generation gaps. Finding interests common to different generations can be a challenge for family members. But visiting a grandparent's pet or having the grandparent witness child and pet together can help a faltering link between oldster and youngster. Playing with an animal allows the older adult to remember similar pleasures during earlier years. Usually, children have few problems engaging in play when an animal is nearby. Frolicking with an animal helps everyone relax. This is healthy activity that can be infectious and fun for all.

For two of my clients, a pet's presence was instrumental in achieving intergenerational harmony. Phillip and Marla came for marital therapy after Marla had had an affair. Phillip, who was fifty, had recently been made vice-president of his computer software company, but his efforts to achieve this goal had placed a strain on the marriage. Marla had been lonely and also worried about turning fifty. When a college sweetheart had come to town, Marla had believed she could turn back the clock. When Phillip learned of her infidelity, he was hurt and angry. They worked hard patching up their neglected relationship. After seven months they began once again to be open and trusting with each other.

But soon after, a new problem emerged. Phillip's father died and they had to decide if his mother should be invited to move in with them. Phillip had never been close to his mother. Complicating the situation was his family credo of keeping a stiff upper lip; in other words, never ask for what you need. Now that Phillip had learned to be honest about his feelings toward his wife and to communicate his needs, he found it easier to be emotionally available to his mother. Both Phillip and Marla felt responsible for the seventy-two-year-old woman, but it was clear they didn't want her to move in and that she didn't want to either. She wanted to rebuild her life with her own friends and hobbies.

Along with financial support, Phillip presented his mother with Johnson, a two-year-old cat. Johnson not only helped to fill the recent void, but his presence in her life brought her into several animal groups that encouraged activity and helped her make new friends. When her great-grandchildren visited during the holidays, Johnson was a major attraction. He proved to be a link to the family. And he helped his mistress find a renewed sense of being needed because of her involvement with the animal projects in the community.

When to Put Pet and Older Parent Together

Several of my patients have asked my advice on when and how they should give pets to their parents. Not every senior citizen wants a pet. But if the interest is there, here are some guidelines for matching a pet to an older relative.

1. Pet ownership for the elderly can be a therapeutic experience. Talk to your relative about what kind of pet would be most appreciated. Oftentimes there is a decided preference for a type of pet owned in the past.

2. Evaluate the home and health of the person who will receive the pet. Some people are allergic to cats and dogs; a different kind of pet, such as a bird, may be a more appropriate offering.

3. Consider the age and the health of the pet. Puppies and kittens may need more initial work than your relative cares to assume. On the other hand, a pet that is old may develop health problems and die suddenly.

4. If the pet is to be given to someone quite elderly, you might need to assume responsibility for its grooming or veterinary care.

5. Look into dog obedience training for retirees, available in some states. This program can be a healthy way to keep your relative active and to make sure the dog is kept under control.

6. Remember that each situation is individual. Be sure to list carefully for your relative all the pros and cons of pet ownership. It could turn out that volunteering at a pet orphanage or being a visiting grandparent to the family dog or cat may best suit your relative's way of life.

SUMMARY

Animals help us enjoy a healthier life. It has been shown that stroking and talking to pets contributes to lower blood pressure and a higher survival rate in heart patients. Our pets remind us to relax and to participate in their love of nature. Walking or training dogs encourages exercise. Pets offer us laughter and solace during times of loss. Their presence gives us a sense of security and safety in times of stress. As we grow older, they keep us from worry and depression. Their playful activity can even close the generation gap and bring families together. They motivate us to become involved in groups within the community. Animals encourage our spirit of youthfulness and remind us that we are always needed.

As we move through the psychological transitions of our lives, we can rely on our animals to support us and love us. In the next chapter we will see what role they play in the development of individuality and in defining a unique sense of self.

CHAPTER TWO

Achieving Individuality

M aking the right choices about work, love relationships, and leisure time is of the greatest importance for young men and women today. But making appropriate choices requires self-knowledge and feelings of self-worth. We must have confidence in ourselves before we can choose effectively, which requires separating from our parents' values and expectations and developing a sense of security about what we want and need as independent individuals. Achieving individuality, then, is the major psychological task that faces everyone as they confront the pleasures and the responsibilities of taking on an adult role in society.

Some look to psychotherapy in this process to counteract hurtful parental criticism or unrealistic parental expectations, which can hold them back from fulfilling their potential as adults. But another, more accessible resource that can help strengthen self-understanding and bolster a shaky sense of self-worth is the companionship and support of a pet therapist. During the process of leaving behind the past to develop an individual identity, pets can serve as warm, receptive teachers. They offer us unconditional love and acceptance as we let go of the familiar — and often restrictive — security of our parents' agenda. They support us through our inevitable mistakes while we search for the path that's right for us.

Achieving individuality can be exciting and satisfying. It can also be lonely and discouraging. In moments of despair, childhood feelings of helplessness often reemerge. Luckily, attitudes, which were learned in the past, can be relearned. We can direct ourselves toward positive feelings and active behavior. Exercises that encourage self-assertion and that work to change a pattern of passivity and failure into one of success sometimes help. From these exercises we can learn to trust ourselves in making decisions and in setting goals. We can define our values and needs as being separate from those of our parents. We can explore our creative potential and find new talent and a new joy in life. There is no age at which we stop learning individuality; it is a dynamic, ongoing process. In this chapter I illustrate my discussion with cases where my patients have been part of this courageous undertaking. In addition, I describe exercises that can be done at home that will direct you on your own path toward individuality.

DEVELOPING A SENSE OF SELF

The process of developing our own distinct identity is the central issue in most contemporary psychology. Jean Piaget, for example, describes the transitional process children go through as they move from a place of safety and security to one of surprise, imbalance, and sometimes anxiety in the journey to adulthood (Jean Piaget, *The Essential Piaget,* ed. Howard E. Gruber and J. Jacques Voneche [New York: Basic Books, 1977]). Growing, then, has both its rewards and its discomforts. We can choose to view this temporary imbalance during the process of growth as troublesome, as a problem, or we can use it as an opportunity to reclaim valuable pieces of our past experience to contribute to our unique personality.

Erik Erikson, another celebrated human development psychologist, views psychological growth as an ongoing quest for identity, during which we continually ask ourselves the question Who am I? As we move through each stage of life, we answer the question of identity temporarily, successfully meeting challenges at each stage. We start to learn in childhood how to trust ourselves and our environment, develop our sense of autonomy and initiative, and gain confidence in our knowledge and learning skills. As adolescents we develop our sexual identity and move into adulthood to meet the challenge of establishing intimacy and contributing to society. If the demands of a particular stage in our development are not met, however, which often happens to some degree, we continue to struggle with that problem in later life (Erik H. Erikson, *Identity and the Life Cycle*, [New York: W. W. Norton, 1979]).

Abraham Maslow, one of the fathers of humanistic psychology, describes growth as a dynamic process we experience throughout life. He believes that we all have the natural potential to become self-actualized, or self-fulfilled, adults. To develop this potential requires self-knowledge and the loving acceptance of others (Abraham H. Maslow, *Toward a Psychology of Being*, 2nd ed. [New York: D. Van Nostrand Co., 1968]).

Carl Rogers, a psychological explorer of human personality, like Maslow, describes our need for a climate of safety and acceptance in which to grow. He tells us of his experience with troubled clients whose negative self-judgments prevent them from making decisions that are consistent with their best interests. When they develop a sense of self-acceptance, however, they learn to accept the validity of their own decisions. Only when we can accept ourselves as we are do we have the foundation for growth (Carl R. Rogers, *Client-Centered Therapy: Its Current Practice, Implications, and Theory* [Boston: Houghton, 1951]).

Frederick Perls, who originated Gestalt therapy, offers the view that each of us has the ability to satisfy our needs by listening to our own experiences. He believes in the values of spontaneity, sensory awareness, emotional responsiveness, enjoyment, self-support, and creativity. His works show that if you are in immediate contact with your experience (he calls it the here and now), you will know what is best for you. By listening to yourself you can learn to make decisions and take responsibility for your life. In other words, you can become your own teacher and guide in leading a satisfying, fulfilling existence (Fritz Perls, *Gestalt Therapy Verbatim* [Lafayette, Calif.: Real People Press, 1969]).

All of these creative pioneers of psychological growth, and scores of others, believe that psychological health is built on the foundation of self-knowledge and the feeling of self-worth that comes from experimenting with life choices. They agree that the process of growth is at times difficult, but that we have within us the potential to learn self-support and confidence by trusting our own experience.

In the pages that follow, stories of how my patients stopped to assess their present difficulty in relation to past unfinished experiences illustrate this process of developing self-understanding. The clients I describe were interested in, and open to, the idea of using pets in therapy. They found the animal's presence to be a supportive part of their struggle to achieve psychological independence. In fact, each found a way to gain inner strength by using a pet as a catalyst to bring into play his or her own natural skills at psychological problem solving. Each found a laboratory for learning by working with their own pet at home in structured therapy. They evolved a sense of self-support and acceptance, and gave themselves permission to be vulnerable, open, and creative. They discovered that their four-footed therapist could serve as a guide to uncovering their own healthy, creative potential for personal growth. You will see how you can have the same experience with your pet.

STRENGTHENING SELF-WORTH

The sense of self-worth—how smart, capable, attractive, and lovable we think we are—develops in childhood as we experience our parents', peers', teachers', and siblings' perceptions of, and judgments about, us. If those around us valued our opinions and feelings and encouraged us to experiment and learn freely—making mistakes along the way—it is easier for us as adults to have faith in our decisions. On the other hand, if those around us were overly critical and demanding, and we learned that it was wrong to feel and act differently from prescribed attitudes, we may well have developed ambivalence and a lack of confidence in our ability to make choices.

Of course few of us had ideal parents who knew how to demonstrate optimal love and recognition for our worth and individuality, especially when they thought what we were doing was wrong. As a result, many of us find ourselves not trusting our own perceptions and feelings as adults. Our ability to use our experience to make intelligent and appropriate decisions is clouded by these unresolved conflicts from childhood. Until we learn to separate our parents' expectations from what we really want as adults, we tend to feel confused, frustrated, angry, or depressed at important junctures in our lives.

Discarding Parental Messages

A critical part of becoming an independent adult is finding out which parental messages from childhood no longer fit. In examining our attitudes and behavior, we learn that we are often unknowingly operating from old, inappropriate scripts. The job of the individual wishing to grow is to lay aside these scripts and develop faith in his or her own ability to make choices.

If we grew up with parents who had unreasonable expectations of us and criticized instead of praised, we, as adults, develop the same harsh critic inside ourselves. As we lived with that constant, nagging deprecation, we internalized that critical voice. As adults we now have a built-in prod to become more and more "perfect." Because we cannot ever satisfy this expectation, we develop a persistent emotional hunger and get little satisfaction out of work or relationships. We move through our daily experiences listening for outside sources of validation of our worth, which only increases our feelings of dependencey and dissatisfaction. We try to be what we think others expect of us rather than letting our own instincts tell us who we really are.

If this persists we can experience a lack of self-respect, with its attendant anxiety and feelings of hopelessness. Our sense of helplessness generates the belief that we cannot effectively cope with everyday problems. At this point we must stop and reassess our sense of self-worth. For some people the presence of a pet breaks into this moment of helplessness. We now can turn to our pet therapist to help us move on. We can use our pet to gain insight into our problem or to heal emotional voids or to break out of a self-destructive pattern.

Relearning Self-Worth

For people who feel worthless, it is imperative to reacquire a feeling of self-worth. If it has been discarded as a result of parental behavior, some believe it will never resurface, but this is not true: self-worth can be relearned.

Doreen's case illustrates how feelings of worthlessness are a learned response, and how feelings of self-acceptance can be restored. Doreen blamed her ex-husband for her feelings of depression and dissatisfaction. She had married at twenty-one to escape her critical, demanding mother, believing that marriage would validate her sense of worth. But the seeds of self-doubt had taken root deep within. During her adolescence she had rebelled against her mother by experimenting with alcohol and sex. When she had left home, her mother had told her that no man would ever love and respect her.

Doreen had married the first man who had proposed, and had proceeded to make unreasonable demands and criticize him for the twelve years of their marriage. When he had become sexually impotent, she had insisted he go for help. Within a year he had left her for another woman. Doreen had felt crushed by this rejection and remembered her mother's prediction that no man would love her. She came to my office struggling with the painful experiences of her life.

When I first suggested she could work on herself by talking to her cat, Mathilda, Doreen was skeptical. She knew how much Mathilda loved her, but she didn't see the connection between how unloved she felt inside and what her cat thought of her. I brought my Burmese cat Casey to the office so Doreen could practice working with a pet therapist. She put Casey on her lap and slowly began to stroke his fur. I suggested she tell Casey some warm and loving statements about what a good cat he was. As Doreen spoke to him he began to purr, and Doreen got an immediate reinforcement that he cared about her and heard the positive words. But it wasn't just Casey who heard the love and acceptance. It was also the little girl inside Doreen, who had always waited to hear those words from her mother, but had waited in vain. Now the message came through, and Doreen was on her way to learning a positive sense of self-worth.

A negative self-image is learned — and can be unlearned. Doreen's experience in my office, and later practicing with her own cat at home, began to change how she felt about herself. Instead of hearing the old, inappropriate, negative messages, she learned to take in positive messages from both herself and, ultimately, others.

Reclaiming our sense of worth takes time. First, we must gain clarity about the old messages that have been taken in, and then we must prepare a space for our own natural perceptions. Part of the support for this process comes from contact with a pet, who accepts us without reservation and encourages our movement toward a personal self-expression by reminding us that we are lovable and unique and deserve to enjoy the positive, healthier side of ourselves.

Sometimes people deny they have problems with feelings of self-worth. Another patient, Rick, was a good example of this behavior. Rick was an articulate business economist who, when still quite young, had acquired a reputation for sharp, intuitive judgments in finance and corporate merger. He had completed Harvard Business School and immediately begun to execute his life plan, which included starting his own firm, marrying an intelligent and attractive woman, and living in a beautiful home. When he reached his thirty-fifth birthday, Rick began to experience persistent stomach pains that his physician diagnosed as psychosomatic and suggested that Rick find out more about his emotional needs. When he came to me, he was skeptical and short on time but willing to see what he could do to feel better.

"I've spent my life learning the laws of business and economy, and I've always tried to take the practical approach to solving problems. I don't see how I managed to end up in a shrink's office. I hope we can get this settled by the first of next month. I have a merger coming up out of town that will take an enormous amount of my attention." Rick briefly glanced at Lorelei, who had given him a warm welcome when he came in.

As Rick described his life, I could hear that it had been years since he had stopped to take stock of his feelings or wonder why he strove with such obsessiveness to succeed. As he described his childhood, the demands of his parents to have a well-educated, outstanding eldest son began to come clear. His father had made and lost fortunes, and the family had expected and encouraged only those parts of Rick's character that had fit their ideal, the parts that had made him the hard-working, perfectionist, successful financier that he was. This one-sided development had made for an inadequate foundation for Rick's sense of self-worth.

"It seems like another lifetime when I was young. I don't know what would happen to me if I stopped listening to financial reports and started listening to myself. I've always known how to be even more than what was expected of me. I guess there were moments a long time ago when I didn't have to be on target. But when were they?"

Rick stopped talking for the first time since he had entered the room, and in the silence Lorelei raised her head for a pat. Knowing that Rick was fond of dogs and enjoyed Lorelei, I suggested that he experiment with role-playing by pretending that Lorelei could understand his words. With some urging, he allowed himself to drop his efficient, problem-solving mentality, and reached down to talk to her. "You know, Lorelei, I used to have a dog as big as you when I was eight. The two of us would go camping together. He was a good friend when I wanted to get out of the house and be myself."

Talking to Lorelei allowed Rick to relive some of his boyhood memories, before he had become the perfect student and the perfect son. That was Rick's first experience at letting down his defenses and allowing himself to reexperience his feelings about his parents' high hopes for him. He remembered that as a child, he had been afraid that he could never live up to the ideal that he had believed his parents wanted him to fulfill. He had spent the past twenty years of his life striving to keep ahead of his perfectionist internal executive. His body had finally communicated its distress, and Rick was forced to take time out to examine his way of life.

Being with Lorelei each week was a warm and moving experience for him. She had no expectations or demands, and he felt loved not for his achievement but for himself. He decided to buy a dog of his own, and purchased a Labrador retriever he named Socrates. Later Rick told me that Socrates helped him remember his early sense of freedom and moments of joy. Through therapy and some exercises with his dog, Rick was able to make peace with his demanding internal overseer. He was able to see that he didn't need to be perfect in order to execute his life plan. His body, including his stomach, relaxed as he learned to enjoy the career for which he had such talent. Both Lorelei and Socrates encouraged him to accept his imperfections and his separateness from parental expectations. With this self-acceptance, Rick achieved a true sense of self-worth.

Responding to our parents' or teachers' aspirations for us without the balance of our own dreams can set up an overly demanding "parent" in our emotional message system. It can be especially difficult to recognize the problem if we have fulfilled many of these hopes and are rewarded by the approval of our family and friends. It may take a stressful problem in our life or our body to make us focus attention on more personal, less visible values. Animals can offer us this time and love as we reevaluate our needs. They can help us return to earlier, nore natural values and reaffirm our feelings of self-worth.

How we perceive our present sense of self-worth and self-confidence is the product of the long journey we take from childhood through adulthood. We develop self-esteem by facing life's normal problems and frustrations as we achieve self-direction. But self-direction requires separating our needs from those of our parents. For some of us this may require a return to the past and a reexperiencing of our inner child. When we make this visit, we have our adult intelligence and experience and, for some of us, the supportive acceptance of our pet therapist.

The following exercise is designed to enhance the natural ways that animals can show us affection, remind us that we are lovable, and serve as a link to our positive childhood experiences. Our pets can be a tool that teaches us how to replenish our diminished feelings of self-worth.

Exercise Two: Regaining Self-Worth

This is an exercise to increase your sense of self-worth. Practice it with your pet as often as you like. It will help erase the nagging voice of self-doubt that we all hear inside our heads from time to time. It will also serve as a guide to the child of our past and help us find the way to the self-acceptance that we are all capable of achieving.

1. Find a quiet place to be with your pet. You may discover that being outdoors is most conducive for your pet therapy work.

2. Reach over and give your pet a gentle hug. Stroke its fur, letting it feel from your touch just how special it is to you.

3. Look into its eyes and tell it how important it is to you. Praise its looks, its character, its intelligence.

4. *Let yourself experience the warm, loving message you are giving to your pet. Close your eyes and, as you continue stroking, say the affectionate words again, adding some phrases of your own that communicate love. Notice that your pet is listening and appreciating your voice and your touch. (This is a positive, loving message to your pet and also to the child that remains inside you. Many of our needs come from that place, as a consequence of what we experienced as children.)*

5. *Now continue the exercise by letting yourself remember a warm, happy, free time in your childhood when you felt good about yourself over some special incident. It may have been playing with a friend or an animal, a special occasion at school or at home, or just a magic moment of being in tune with your own sense of aliveness.*

6. *Share that experience out loud with your pet.*

You now have established a link between a current experience of warmth and acceptance and the good feeling of the child of your past. This exercise works because it puts us in contact with a basic psychological need that all human beings have: the need for touch.

Being stroked and held is the first message of love from mother to child. It is a powerful message of unconditional acceptance and nurturance. By stroking and talking to your pet, you are nurturing the child of yesterday. By remembering the happy time you had in the past, you are linking a feeling of self-esteem to your present experience of pet therapy. During this exercise you probably will feel a warm glow of love.

Working with our pet therapist allows us to verbalize and try out new ways of perceiving and experiencing ourselves. We allow ourselves to be open, to be vulnerable, and to feel ourselves loved. In moments of conflict and need, our pet offers no advice, no recrimination, and no judgment. We experience support to deal with the frustration and fear that often emerges with new problems. We find ourselves confronted with the stress of continual life decisions, some of which bring back self-doubts and a lack of self-confidence. But we need not face this process of decision making alone. We have a four-footed therapist as our companion.

MAKING THE RIGHT CHOICES

What career should I pursue? Whom should I love? How should I spend my time? How should I spend my money? These are questions that start in early childhood and last a lifetime. As we saw in the preceding section, the foundation for making choices starts in the separation process from our parents. If our earlier decisions were made in accordance with family values and we believed our parents knew what was right for us, the experience of breaking away can be frightening. The pattern of dependency starting with our parents may persist with friends or our spouse. If we remain in this safe, static pattern, we become bored and restless, and may seek to blame others because we feel like a prisoner.

On the other hand, rebellion against parental values can keep us in a continual battle with our parents that we carry throughout our adult lives. If we do not examine this perhaps age-encrusted internal struggle, we have not allowed ourselves a true choice.

In the struggle to develop self-confidence and independence, we can turn to our animals for support. They can help us to keep focused on our own personal experience, accept feelings of hesitancy and inevitable mistakes, and find a path to natural growth. Their presence and unfaltering affection helps us trust in our ability to choose for ourselves, and allows us to believe that we deserve pleasure, love, and success.

Sorting Things Out Before Making Your Choice

As my patients struggle to make the right choices, they often look to me for the answers. I hear such quesitons as, "Should I give up my boyfriend?" "Should I marry this woman?" "Am I right in wanting a divorce?" "Is it the right time to buy a house?" "Should I have a baby?" and countless others. But the crux of the problem is not the choice itself, but how to make the choice. A sense of self-direction is inhibited by a lack of self-knowledge and self-confidence.

Sylvia, twenty-seven, had married her husband during his last year of law school. When he had passed the bar exam, she had hoped their financial struggle was at an end. Their courtship had been romantic and the decision to marry had been made quickly. Sylvia's parents had opposed the timing of the marriage, believing that she had not allowed herself the opportunity to finish her own education and explore a career. Two years after the marriage, Sylvia came to therapy bored with her life and dissatisfied with her husband.

"I'm tired of being there for Don and having to work as a secretary while he builds up a law practice. When I talk about stopping work to have a baby, he insists we wait for some financial security in our lives. I'm sick of doing what Don thinks is best for me. I'm getting older and I think I should have a baby before I'm thirty. Mother had a difficult time with her last pregnancy, and I don't want to have a problem like that. Why should I set my parenting schedule to suit Don's career when he is never around for me? Maybe I should leave him and let him take care of his career without me. I really don't know where to turn or what I should do, but I feel angry and depressed with my life."

With this outpouring of anger and disappointment, Sylvia stopped for breath and waited for my advice. She felt helpless to do anything other than fight with her husband or leave. This was an old pattern, which she had created as a child. She first would go along with what her parents felt was right, and then become dissatisfied and angry. Blaming others for the problem, she would make some gesture of retaliatory rebellion without waiting to assess her options.

It was a long struggle for Sylvia to examine her life and how she had been trying to satisfy her needs. In the months that followed, she confronted her fear of not knowing what to do and the frustration of not having an immediate answer. It was hard for her to live with the anxiety of this ambiguity, but she got help in the process from Lorelei, who is by nature a calm and patient dog. As Sylvia went back and reexperienced her choices, she used Lorelei to enact role-playing exercises with her parents. Before she could make a valid decision about whether to continue her marriage, she needed to understand her own needs and how she had avoided the responsibility for making decisions in the past. She had been caught in the bind of either adopting her parents' values and following their advice or blindly opposing them. She needed to find herself before she could define her role as wife and mother. In this sorting-out process, she learned to talk out her feelings at home with her German shepherd, Emily, whose warm, motherly qualities helped Sylvia learn how to parent herself and find the courage to make her own decisions.

The case of Ken is another example of a patient learning to individuate. Like Sylvia, Ken was forced to examine his own needs and values. Ken had graduated with a master's degree in business administration and joined his father's successful electrical parts company. As a teenager Ken had worked summers in his father's factory and earned praise for being hard-working and dependable. He had not, however, allowed himself a normal period of adolescent rebellion. As he was the only son, his parents had looked forward to the day he would take over the business. A few years after Ken had joined the company, his father had developed health problems that had prevented him from continuing his active role in the daily operations of the firm. As a result Ken had become more involved in directing the policy and financial structure of the growing corporation.

At thirty-seven Ken had begun to experience daily anxiety attacks, and he frequently suffered from nightmares. Eventually he was forced to seek the cause of these symptoms. That's when he came to me for therapy. As Ken described his life to me, it was easy to understand why he was successful in working with people. He was sensitive, conscientious, and tried to take on all of the problems around him. He had always been considered a good son, and both parents depended on his energy and attention. Unfortunately, in avoiding his submerged rebellion, he had not been attentive to his own need to make a choice for himself.

During one session Ken described a particularly poignant dream. In it he was caught in an elevator in his father's factory that was stuck between floors. He pounded on the elevator doors and pushed switches, trying desperately to get out. No matter which button he pushed, nothing happened. He shouted for help, but the workers stayed by their tables, hearing nothing. Ken started to tremble as he remembered the dream. "I panicked at the end of the dream. I had gone through every possible electrical procedure, and it felt like I had shouted for hours but no one could hear me."

Hearing the pain in his voice, Delilah came over to offer her support. He reached down to pet her, feeling the security of her warm head. I asked Ken to play out the parts of his dream and talk to Delilah as if he were each element in the story. I turned off the lamp by my chair, allowing only diffused sunlight into the room. Ken began speaking in the first person, present tense. He told Delilah, "I am an elevator caught in my father's factory, and I cannot get up or down. I am the worker who attends only to his job and hears no cry for help. I am machinery that does its tasks and never stops. I am a stuck place in an elevator shaft." His voice sounded very young and helpless. His trembling returned. Then I asked him to call again for help as if he were back in the dream. As he did, Delilah came running over and put a paw on his hand. He put his head down near her and began to cry. This was the beginning of many difficult sessions in Ken's search for his own needs and sense of direction. He would learn with Delilah that when he really expressed his need for help, he could be heard.

Ken worked for over a year to examine his personal needs and how he had avoided expressing those needs. He learned how much of himself he had given over to his family. He continued to work on his dreams, using Delilah to help him play out the different aspects of himself. He also practiced this technique at home with his beagles, Mutt and Jeff, who encouraged him to be playful and to listen to himself.

Reexamining Our Choices

If we follow too closely the path of our parents, it's easy to find ourselves feeling imprisoned, like Ken did in his dream about the elevator shaft. This shields us from exploring what we want for ourselves. Even if we do consider alternatives, the possibilities of failure or loss of our parents' approval is always there. Following our family's map may give us a feeling of predictability, but we miss the excitement and aliveness of our own exploration.

Making life choices about love, work, leisure, and creativity challenges us to listen attentively to all parts of our personality. The decisions we make in our early years may need to be reexamined as adults. It's perfectly normal to long for a place of safety and familiarity and resent giving up love and approval from parents or a spouse for our behavior. But there is a competing natural desire to separate ourselves as individuals. As we achieve this individuation, we gain a sense of control and confidence. Talking directly about our fears and discovering the attitudes that we have hidden from ourselves brings about a growing integration of our personality. It takes time, faith, and creativity to focus on this process. As we make these discoveries, we can rely on the help of our four-footed therapists.

The following exercise is a self-awareness process designed to help you define your identity. By practicing role playing with your pet, you can see your perceptions about, and roles in, your family system. You can also see the stages at which you made choices without being consciously aware of them. This exercise can bring you a clarified sense of what influences your choices today, and it offers you the opportunity to experiment with different self-perceptions. Of course role playing does not require the use of a pet, but having an attentive animal at your side can motivate you into doing the exercise and can give you positive reinforcement when you have completed it.

Exercise Three: Who am I? — Making the Right Choices

1. Sit in a quiet place with your pet, and let yourself experience a moment of relaxed contact with your animal therapist. Breathe deeply and be aware of your senses — what you see, hear, feel, touch, and taste — at this moment. Tell your pet what you are experiencing.

2. Then tell your pet, "This is what I am like right now. What I would like to be at this moment is . . . ." Complete your statement with whatever self-description comes to mind.

3. Then pretend to be your pet and imagine what it is sensing and what it may like at this moment. It may be hungry and want a snack, or it may be restless and want to play. This part can be fun, so relax and enjoy the fantasy.

4. Now that you have warmed up your ability to project and pretend, imagine that you are your parent of the same sex — your mother if you are a woman and your father if you are a man. From that parent's perspective, talk about your child (yourself) as you view your child today. Describe yourself, your achievements, your failures, your ability to love, and whatever other characteristics come to mind. Have your parent describe any changes he or she would like you to make in your life today — that is, a better relationship, a different job, more money, more friends, a different attitude toward the family, a different place to live, and so on. How do these comments sound to you?

5. Tell your pet therapist whether that perception and those wishes match your self-perception and wishes today. If they don't correspond to your thinking, you have identified something your same-sex parent believes or values that doesn't fit for you. Examine it more closely by repeating out loud to your pet what you are like and what you want for yourself, and then your parent's views. What are the differences and similarities? If they are numerous you may need to write them on two lists, and examine them out loud with your animal therapist. Is there an overlap between your thinking and your parent's thinking?

6. Finally, end the exercise by having your pet give you a positive message about how it perceives you and what it wants for you today. (Imagine what it would tell you and say it aloud.) Take this affectionate message into your experience as you and your pet sit together for a moment longer.

7. When you feel ready, you may repeat this exercise, this time playing the role of your opposite-sex parent.

You have carried these parental beliefs and wishes in your head for a long time, so be patient with yourself as you sort them out on paper or say them aloud to your pet. When you have clarified your thinking and your parents' thinking, you are ready to begin to make the right choices for yourself.

This exercise works because it permits you to relax and fantasize in the supportive presence of your pet. It frees your logical mind and habitual perceptions and encourages you to explore your parents' attitudes as you have experienced them. Then, using the positive, accepting relationship with your pet, it allows you to reshape and make more satisfying your self-image and to define your current choices.

Projecting your awareness onto your pet and letting yourself fantasize is a way of gaining knowledge about the perceptions that shaped your life and influenced your choices. It can stretch your ability to evaluate yourself and increase your confidence in making daily, as well as long-term, choices. With this new awareness and knowledge, you are ready to look at another dimension of achieving individuality: how to get what you want.

GETTING WHAT YOU WANT

A lack of self-confidence and little experience in assertiveness can cause a person to be placating and ineffectual in social and work relationships. Like feelings of self-worth and the ability to make decisions, the ability to be assertive and act in our own best interests is learned behavior. If we were lucky, our parents provided role models that showed us how to get what we wanted through appropriate behavior. If we lacked models, we may feel controlled and powerless in situations that require us to be clear and assertive.

Well-meaning parents and teachers sometimes encourage quiet, polite, passive behavior in children and reward them for not making their desires known. If we have undergone this kind of conditioning, we may find ourselves excessively solicitous, soft-spoken, agreeable, inhibited adults, powerless to get what we want. We are afraid of spontaneity and firmness. This behavior is often linked to low self-esteem and an inability to make effective choices. If we believe our only choice is to give in, our feelings of self-esteem depreciate even more.

The attitude of accommodation and "making no waves" springs from the fear that we will lose the safety, love, and approval that our pleasing, passive behavior elicits. We believe that if we show our sense of independence and say what we want, we will no longer be appreciated and accepted by family, friends, colleagues, or even strangers. In this vacuum of reality testing, we imagine the possibility of frightening confrontations and painful arguments. We see ourselves not knowing what to say, looking foolish, and, worst of all, making a mistake that cannot be changed.

Learn to be Assertive!

The fear of experimenting and expressing differences can be overcome by learning the tools of self-assertion. Practicing with a pet therapist can reshape our behavior, teach us the skills of effectively dealing with others, and develop our sense of confidence that we can get what we want.

One memorable experience when I first acquired my dogs, Lorelei and Delilah, was taking them to obedience training classes. I was forced to make clear, firm statements about what I wanted from them. I was not seeking their approval or attempting to please them. I was not able to reason, persuade, or be seductive. It was all black and white, no in between. My body language, tone of voice, and words had to correspond. I was able to evaluate my communication technique immediately, because I received a reward for what succeeded. There is no place for avoidance or passivity in dog obedience training.

Dog obedience training is founded on the classic studies of conditioning and learning. The dog's behavior is shaped by responding to a system of reward and punishment. It is conditioned to obey its owner by getting either enthusiastic praise or a jerk of the collar and a strong "No." As the process continues, the dog owner is also being conditioned to a pattern of behavior. The owner learns to focus on the dog, and to make clear, firm commands. The owner is rewarded for his or her efforts by having an obedient dog. Both owner and pet are conditioned: the dog learns to behave and the owner learns a sense of his or her own power and authority.

Linda was one of my patients who relearned self-assertion by taking her dog to obedience classes. She was a twenty-six-year-old research analyst who rarely took a firm stand on anything. She did not recieve the salary raises her work deserved, and when someone was needed to work overtime, she was always selected. On a date she would try too hard to please the man, and would later wonder why he didn't call again.

Linda had grown up the middle child in a family that had rewarded her "unselfishness," consideration, and ability to fit into other people's priorities. Her parents were preoccupied with their own demanding schedules and with the declining condition of their marriage. There was a paucity of love for the children. Consequently, Linda developed an eagerness to please and tried to get attention and approval whenever she could. Her father, who gave her more time than her mother, encouraged her to follow what he believed were the best values for his daughter: he taught her to be courteous, considerate, and obliging with both peers and adults. Linda loved and admired her father, and so patterned her behavior to his ideals. Unfortunately, at twenty-six she found herself frustrated, unhappy, and unable to get what she wanted.

At the beginning of one session with me, Linda heard me tell Lorelei to sit down and lie quietly. She knew I loved my dogs, and was taken aback by the firm, no-nonsense tone of my voice. Linda always spoke softly and found it hard to clearly articulate what she meant. I suggested she try some obedience commands, and she was surprised to see how quickly Lorelei obeyed her.

"She listened to me when I said no. I can't believe it!"

Linda felt a surge of excitement, and I suggested that she experiment, exaggerating the tone of her voice and how strong she could sound as she gave Lorelei more commands. Linda practiced standing on a chair and looking down at Lorelei. Then she took

Lorelei's collar and said in a clear, firm voice, "Lorelei, I am in charge here and you will do what I tell you." Linda had gotten in touch with her sense of power by learning how to be "top dog."

In the sessions that followed, Linda relived her earlier family relationships and began to understand the ways she had avoided working to get what she wanted. She had abdicated her responsibility and then wondered why she could not get what she wanted. Her practice with Lorelei helped her to learn this about herself, and she decided to get a puppy and learn more about asserting herself at home. She selected a Doberman pinscher, whom she named Victoria, and took her to obedience training classes. Linda continued her work in therapy, and through it and her weekly obedience classes, she developed a new sense of confidence. This feeling of strength then transferred to other situations in which she needed to assert herself. She discovered that she could be respected and appreciated not by blindly following her parents' rules but by assuming responsibility for the satisfaction of her own needs.

Darrell was another patient who had problems asserting himself. A forty-one-year-old psychiatrist, he could solve problems in his office but couldn't say no to his critical and controlling fiancée. She chose the time and location of their ski trips, picked the gourmet cooking classes they should attend, and even selected the material for his imported tweed jackets. She was a marketing executive who couldn't leave her professional management role out of their relationship.

"Why are women never satisfied with the way I am? I never seem to please them." Darrell described growing up with a quiet, peace-loving father and a demanding, critical mother who taught high school. He had worked hard at achieving success, but had never gotten his mother's approval. She had always expected more of him than he was able to offer. From his father he had learned to be passive in a relationship. And he was still working to satisfy his disapproving mother, now in the guise of attempting to please his girlfriend.

After Darrell discussed the relationship between his childhood experiences and his lack of self-assertion, he practiced role playing with Lorelei, the more maternal of my two dogs. He pretended that Lorelei was his mother (as if the pet, in the role of mother, could hear and understand him) and expressed his feelings about being thwarted in his desire to please others or himself, in the process recognizing that he was no longer a little boy who needed his mother's approval. He relived a scene from junior high when his mother had rejected his report card because it was "not up to his potential." His voice shook as he remembered his feeling of shame. Then his voice filled with anger as he told his mother she was not the judge of his work. When the exercise was over, Darrell felt excited about his new sense of power. In another session he pretended that Lorelei was his girlfriend, and made forceful statements to her about what he thought she should do and how he thought she should do it. Purposely exaggerating his demands and his authority moved him toward a firmer sense of self-assurance. He moved about the room, speaking gruffly and "throwing his weight around." By then the three of us were having fun, and Darrell, with the help of his dog therapist, had experienced a new role in his life — that of a more assertive man who was self-confident and less dependent on others for approval.

When you say yes but you mean no, you are fooling yourself into believing that others will truly appreciate or love you for this behavior. Staying with this pattern of passive, placating behavior can numb your sense of knowing what you actually want. It can result in not getting the respect you deserve. Dog training can help jolt you out of this self-defeating way of relating.

Animal obedience training classes, which I find highly effective in dealing with passivity and an avoidance of self-responsibility, are available at most public parks. They usually last eight to ten weeks, are inexpensive, and can be a good place to experiment with assertive behavior. Your puppy or dog can start a basic course, and you can learn to be firm and clear about what you want.

Along with dog obedience classes, your dog or cat can, in the privacy of your home, help you practice with your self-assertion training. The following exercise will help you explore new behavior and reshape your self-confidence.

Exercise Four: Role Playing Self-Assertion

1. Find a quiet place with lots of room and a straight-backed chair with no padding on the back. Sit in the chair and feel the support of the upright, firm back.

2. *Turn to your animal therapist and describe aloud several situations in your life when you felt you let yourself be passive and did not assert what you wanted.*

3. *Choose one of these episodes to act out. It may be a daunting situation at work where you did not clearly state that you wanted a raise or specific recognition for what you did, a friendship based on always what the other person wanted to do, a love relationship where you did not clearly state what you needed, or some other remembered failure where you did not get what you needed.*

4. *When you have made your choice of a situation, your pet will act the role of the person with whom you couldn't be assertive. Start by being as passive and dependent as you can, exaggerating the softness of your voice, assuming a compromising posture, and being totally sweet, vague, and helpless.*

5. *Now pretend your animal is the other person, and imagine what strong, clear, specific, and self-assured statements would come from that position. Hear how the person expects to get what is requested. How does that assertive role sound to you? Ask your pet how it feels to be so powerful, and imagine its enthusiastic answer.*

6. *Now play the same situation from another point of view. You will talk to the same person, but this time act aggressive, overbearing, and loud. Stalk around the room, shaking your fist, throwing back your shoulders, glaring, and demanding, so your body gestures communicate anger and power. This time imagine your animal is a sweet, helpless, insecure person who is afraid to answer you back. Now how did all that aggressive power feel? Ask your pet what it was like to play that helpless part, and imagine its frustrated answer. You have now played two ends of a behavioral spectrum. Both are exaggerated and inaccurate in terms of your everyday experience, but you have stretched and experimented with your behavior.*

7. *Sit on the straight-backed, firm chair and talk to your pet as the same assertive person in step 5. In a clear, calm voice, state what you think and want and need from the person the pet represents. Then state how you expect to get it. When you have finished, ask your pet how it felt about you as it listened. Imagine its answer of respect and its belief in your clarity and confidence. This last position is the appropriate middle ground. It will give you a feeling of centeredness for your real life encounters.*

Repeat this exercise with different unsuccessful situations from the past, but each time select one to resolve in real life during the following week. After the real life encounter, come back to your pet and evaluate what worked and what didn't. (For the points that didn't work, you may have to clarify with your pet therapist again exactly what you wanted.) How did you feel talking to the real person in your life? Do you need to practice the exercise again? Let your pet give you lots of praise for your effort, and you will be ready to try more self-assertive acts in your life.

Achieving what we want and being self-assertive is a creative, positive act, not a destructive or aggressive one. There is always risk involved in stretching ourselves and trying out new behavior. Dog obedience training and role playing self-assertion give you the rehearsal for dealing with obstacles in your life. Using your pet to practice self-assertion increases your chances for success when facing a real life test.

As you gain increasing skills for changing behavioral patterns, making decisions, and satisfying needs, you are ready to learn about another facet of growth and individuality — achieving your potential as a fully realized individual.

ACHIEVING YOUR POTENTIAL

Building a career and raising a family is a full-time responsibilty for much of our adult lives. When children are self-sufficient and when we have attained the professional achievement we have worked for so diligently, a moment arrives when we ask ourselves, Is this all there is? At this stage of developing individuality, my patients come not with the struggle of separating from parents or the hesitancy of self-doubts, but with the emerging internal demand that they want and deserve more. They feel a deepening need for self-exploration and creative expression, a natural drive to become fully realized individuals.

Abraham Maslow described the self-actualized person, or fully realized individual, as one who is productive, makes good use of his or her time, and is open to the full enjoyment of life. When we reach this stage of life, we tend to express a new creativity. We may develop a different career, discover a new dimension to our intimate relationships, or realize the need to find a more rewarding one. We may find self-expression in art, music, movement, or writing as we explore the possibilities of work and play (Abraham

H. Maslow, *Toward a Psychology of Being*, 2nd ed. [New York: D. Van Nostrand Co., 1968]).

Finding Self-Fulfillment

The stage of achieving one's potential is a stage of rediscovery, a broadening of our capacity to enjoy life at both work and play. We have learned to trust our unique individuality. We are not afraid of taking risks. We move toward a deepening understanding of what will be fulfilling. In this process our animal therapists can encourage our ability to listen to our own nature, and support us in periods of reassessing our life and making changes.

Two of my patients illustrate this need for finding a richer sense of self-fulfillment. Neither had problems with feelings of self-worth or achievement, but still they had begun to feel dissatisfied with their lives. They were not satisfied with the growth and coping skills they had developed in earlier years. They each needed to develop a deeper and more creative way of living. In both cases they found the courage to stop and reexamine their already productive lives and to search for a deeper experience in living. They had the self-trust to believe there was more available to them if they would go back and explore earlier, unlived potentials.

Roger was a fifty-three-year-old M.D. with a busy practice and long hours that included nighttime house calls. He served as head of medical evaluation at a hospital, and felt a deep satisfaction with what he had contributed to the field of medicine. He had managed, through hard work and continuing mutual love, to be married for twenty years to the same woman. With both sons in college, he had lately become aware of a feeling that something was still missing from his life.

"I don't seem to ever find time for myself. My schedule is full, and there's always someone waiting for me to solve the next problem. I still love being a doctor, but I have a sense that my life is getting away from me." He reached over and gave Lorelei a solid pat on her body and enjoyed her contented response. It was a rare moment for Roger to stop and let his immediate experience give him pleasure. His sense of discipline had served him well in his work, but he had come to therapy seeking inspiration. He had done a remarkable job of taking care of others, but he had forgotten how to take care of himself.

I suggested he use Lorelei as his initial teacher. First I asked him to act out a short scene for Lorelei, showing her what his day's experience was like. He did this, looking like the mechanical Charlie Chaplin figure from the movie *Modern Times*. Next I asked him to take some deep breaths and remember a time in his childhood when he had been dependent and free of problems. For that moment Lorelei's warm body provided emotional support for Roger as he remembered his relationship with an older brother who had taken him to the beach and carried him out in the waves. This was a carefree, relaxing memory, which in the sessions to come symbolized for Roger his boyhood, his freedom, his sense of play, and a long-suppressed desire for another to take care of him.

In later sessions Roger continued to let himself to emotionally lean on Lorelei and tell her about his boyhood memories. As he experienced these feelings of dependency and reflected on his presently disciplined, controlled life, he stretched his experience of himself and deepened his natural instinct for pleasure and crea-tivity. He remembered his childhood enjoyment of working with clay and began an afternoon class in sculpture (the first afternoons ever away from his office). He discovered that he could let himself experience his relationship with his wife without having to be in charge all the time and solve all the problems. This deepened their intimacy and allowed them to reaffirm their love. Using my dog to psychologically bolster himself, Roger learned to accept other dimensions of his developing self, those of being dependent and being relaxed and find happiness in his creative expression.

Another patient was Sarah who, like many other women, was a successful wife and mother who needed to experience more in order to enrich her personal identity. She came to therapy ready to reexamine her own creative resources and to fulfill this new need. She had been a successful model in New York and had explored her talents as an artist before she had married a movie producer and moved to California. When her two energetic children had been young, Sarah had devoted most of her time to rearing them, in addition to contributing ideas and support to her husband's movie projects. When her children went away to school, the only thing that was uniquely hers was the cat, Minerva. Sarah came to therapy at forty-eight feeling depressed and displaced from her job.

"There must be more to life than seeing your children grow up and helping your husband. I've put on weight in the past few years, and it's hard for me to remember that twenty years ago I was on the cover of *Vogue*. I don't regret having a family, of course, but I've got to do something with the rest of my life that is a personal expression of me. I don't know where the time has gone!"

Sarah talked about her earlier life, and the next time she came to the office, I decided to take advantage of her love of cats and brought my cat Merlin to the session. Even though Sarah spoke longingly of being independent and starting projects of her own, I could hear that she felt anxious and shaky over taking such an unfamiliar step. In this session she put Merlin on the couch next to her, and we constructed a fantasy exercise that would take her back to the magic moments of age sixteen, when she had started her career as a model. She stroked Merlin's fur, closed her eyes, and got in touch with all the feelings of excitement and pleasure she could remember. In her imagination she played out various scenes of what her life might have been if it had gone in different directions. She imagined continuing her modeling career. She pretended to be an artist with a loft in New York City. Finally, she remembered when her children had been infants, and how it had felt to hold them in her arms. Using Merlin as a stage prop, she brought back the experience of being needed and realized again how much she loved her children.

These scenes, as she enacted them in the months of her therapy, gave her a sense of her potential — all the ways she might have lived her life and what she might still do today. This recognition brought to Sarah a clearer sense of herself and the courage to go out in the community and see what was there for her. She also practiced this fantasy work with her own cat. And at the end of a year, she accepted a job at a local hospital, training adolescent girls in grooming, dress, and self-confidence. The job inspired Sarah's own sense of confidence and combined the different talents she possesed as mother, model, and artist. She later returned to school for a degree in social work.

The tools of self-awareness and faith in our own potential develops throughout our lives. But at certain midlife junctures, we have the opportunity to renew our excitement and seek creative experiences. We need to encourage ourselves to stay open to the continuing process of change. As we explore our options, we can look to our pets for support and inspiration. They can serve as a guide to our fantasies, and help us stretch our unused creative muscles. With their help and renewed faith in ourselves, we can achieve our greatest potential.

Following is an exercise to help you actualize your unlived fantasies and dreams. No matter what your job is today — working at a paying job, being a spouse, or being a parent — everyone has this inert potential that is buried in the past. Your pet therapist can help guide you to the fantasy and show you a way to translate the dream into reality. Creating this fantasy does not require a pet, but it is much easier to move into a relaxed state and fantasize while you hold or stroke one. The tactile sensation gives you enough reassuring support to put aside logic and be creative.

Exercise Five: Actualizing Your Dreams

1. Find a quiet place for you and your pet therapist. Sit comfortably and take some deep breaths. Stroke your pet and use a few moments to relax your body. You are going to take a mental journey into your past, looking for some of the sparkle and talent you put aside. Close your eyes, breathe deeply again, and return to the age when you felt happiest and most excited.

2. Visualize youself participating in an activity you used to love doing. Maybe it was art, writing, playing a musical instrument, reading a favorite book, working on a science project in the laboratory, being with someone you admired, or taking care of an animal. Get in touch with the thrill of being involved in that activity. Try to remember your early fantasies about becoming someone special. There may have been a number of these dreams, so let yourself take the time to go through the memories. Be patient with yourself, stroke your pet, and breathe deeply and evenly. Find which dream is the most stirring for you.

3. When you feel you have selected the most powerful fantasy, open your eyes and turn to your pet counselor. Speak to your pet aloud about your dream.

4. Imagine your pet giving you advice on how that dream might fit into your life today. Elaborate on how to translate this fantasy into reality; perhaps you should take a course at night, talk to someone for advice, find something with which you could experiment, resurrect some old notebooks or paints in the garage, rent a piano, or take a weekend to explore nature.

5. Once you've tapped into these dreams, work out a way to make the fantasy part of your life in order to fulfill your creative potential and actualize these unused parts of yourself.

You may need to repeat this exercise at some future time if you should start to lose the dream. Just repeat the steps with your pet, first finding the dream and then putting it into practice. Your animal therapist gives you permission to be inventive and to renew patterns that will expand your individuality. Once you take your need seriously, you can set into motion a different direction for your life.

SUMMARY

Achieving individuality can be a fascinating, satisfying part of the process of growth. It can also be lonely and frightening. You may feel an occasional resurgence of old attitudes of helplessness and hopelessness. Fortunately, attitudes about ourselves can be relearned. We can experiment with self-assertion and change patterns of passivity and failure. We can learn to trust ourselves in making decisions and defining goals. We can separate our values and needs from those of our parents. We can return to our dreams to actualize our full potential. Achieving individuality never stops; it is an ever evolving process.

With this sense of individuality in mind, we are ready to address another dimension in satisfying our emotional needs — developing a love relationship. Knowing and trusting our experience, our needs, and our sense of ourselves gives us the bridge to connect with others.

CHAPTER THREE

Connecting In Love

P ets can play a role in introducing people. For instance, research conducted in London's Hyde Park showed that people walking dogs had more social contacts, were perceived as friendlier, had longer conversations, and took longer walks than people without dogs walking in the same park (Peter R. Messent, "Facilitation of Social Interaction by Companion Animals," paper presented at the International Conference on the Human-Companion Bond, Philadelphia, October 5–7, 1981). For those desiring social connections, a pet may be the ideal catalyst for new friendships.

For some single people, however, meeting others is not the problem. Instead, recognizing the need for love and allowing a relationship to develop can be the major internal struggles for people striving for permanent commitment. Making the right choices and avoiding the wrong ones requires self-confidence, experimentation, openness to evaluating personal patterns in love, and faith in the process of love. When a close relationship does develop, oftentimes men and women become afraid of their feelings of vulnerability and loss of autonomy. And if the relationship begins to deteriorate or breaks up, the partners may feel disoriented and unlovable.

Dealing with disappointment and loss is often done in isolation. Having a supportive pet therapist by your side reminds you that you are not totally alone. A warm, responsive pet, by offering emotional contact, gives its owner the chance to meet others and to experience tenderness and vulnerability, qualities that are prerequisites to accepting the need for love. Pet therapy then can be an ideal way for single people to learn how to make connections and develop relationships. It is equally effective with couples contemplating marriage, because caring for an animal teaches sharing and responsibility, which in turn build trust and foster communication. Because a pet gives clear messages when it needs attention, couples have an ever present model to emulate when they need these same attentions from each other. A pet therapist is also an important factor if the connection doesn't work and couples split up. In this case a pet will offer unconditional support, which in turn will add to feelings of self-esteem. A high level of self-worth is important in connecting with others.

RECOGNIZING THE NEED FOR LOVE

Many single people fight the universal need for love by creating a shell of independence and activity. They hide their warmth and their need for warmth from themselves and others. Women successful in their careers tend to feel conflicted about their need for nurturance. Their work roles do not encourage the softer, open qualities so important in starting and maintaining a relationship. Given the demands of a still male-oriented working world, single women are often driven to compete and achieve, and may leave room for little else.

The single man may find himself caught in a web of his own making, approaching his relationships with women in a superficial, fleeting way. He may worry about losing his autonomy if he commits himself to a relationship. But what he is actually protecting himself from is the intimacy that could occur if he let himself stop and experience the genuine contact that is available to him.

These women and men may also be afraid of their feelings of vulnerability, which may be extreme because of unresolved feelings of dependency on a parent. These feelings may have been covered over for years. Consequently, they find themselves in an internal struggle, seeking something they are afraid to reveal in themselves. This struggle requires a great deal of energy and does not achieve the desired effect — finding love. Eventually, the anxiety inherent in the conflict creeps out and displays itself. At this point the animal therapist can intervene in the battle and help a person focus on the genuine needs at the core of the anxiety.

The case of Marlene is typical of the way many successful young people hide their need for love from themselves. Marlene was thirty-one, recently divorced, and working hard to be independent. She went to aerobics classes four times a week, attended plays and concerts alone, and occasionally had dinner with a girlfriend. Marlene was a disciplined eater, devoted to exercise and health, but although she tended to her physical needs, she ignored her emotional ones. Despite her efforts at achieving self-sufficiency, Marlene was waking up at night, shaking and frightened. She didn't know where her anxiety was coming from. Her performance as a television director had begun to suffer. That's when she came to me for help.

Marlene tried to bring the same self-control into therapy that she had programmed into her life. We had been talking for a few months, but hadn't tapped the roots of Marlene's anxiety. Then I decided to introduce one of my pet therapists into the session. Knowing Marlene liked cats, I brought Clancy to her three o'clock session, curious to see how he might help her with the process.

"I hate the way my mother clings to me and tries to make me feel guilty when I don't call her. She may have controlled my father while he was alive, but I refuse to let her get to me. Even when Daddy was in the hospital, she tried to manipulate the family and play the martyr."

Clancy crawled onto her lap as she described her strained relationship with her mother. As she continued I could hear that she fought her sadness with the same discipline she used in her 10K runs.

"Tell me about the last time you visited your father," I said.

Marlene started a review of her father's medical statistics. Her voice quavered as she told me that her father had known he was dying. On their last day together, he had spoken of how pleased he was with her success and how proud he was of her. She stroked Clancy and he responded with a purr. For that instant holding Clancy was safer than talking to me. After a moment she continued, "I didn't realize how much I still missed him."

Marlene then realized that the unresolved loss of her father had been breaking through her regimented life during the night. It was a moment of insight that had been encouraged by a warm, responsive presence. Marlene had finally permitted herself to experience the grief of losing her father. This brought into her awareness her need for affection and nurturance. The anxiety that was causing her sleeplessness and fear served no further purpose because the battle inside her had stopped. This was the beginning of her work to know and accept her needs. She bought herself a kitten and at the same time began to allow more spontaneity into her overly structured life.

Gregg's case is another example of how a single person's way of life can mask a need for love. After graduating from a local university, Gregg had started a small construction company and built it into one of the largest in the state. Although he prided himself on his work, he left no time to attend to his inner needs. As he approached forty he couldn't understand how he could still be alone and unattached. After all, he was successful, handsome, talented at sports, and looked younger than his thirty-nine years. He had been engaged several times, but he had never made it to the altar. His most recent fiancée had bluntly told him that it was obvious to her that there was no place in his life for her. With a nagging sense of disquietude, Gregg entered therapy to figure out how he could improve his life.

"I don't know why I'm still single. I fall in love, get engaged, and think I have just what I've been looking for. Then as we begin to plan for the future, something happens. The whole thing falls apart. Love is the one thing that I just can't get a handle on. I don't understand women. They say they want to be taken care of. But then when I take charge, they complain that I act like a dictator instead of a lover."

I could see that Gregg's independence could be attractive, yet it was equally apparent that it could stymie a woman who wanted to be close to him. Gregg sat for a minute in puzzled silence. He reached down to Lorelei, who was sitting nearby, and gave her a brief pat. I seized the moment and suggested he explore his family relationships. But instead Gregg launched into an analysis of what was wrong with the women to whom he had become close, and what he should have done differently. It became clear to me that

Gregg had a formula that was successful in his business: he devised a plan, took charge, made a decision, and relied on his own resources. But this formula wasn't working for him in love. His protective independence didn't allow a place for his girlfriends any more than it would permit Lorelei or me to interrupt his tight agenda in a therapy session.

After a few more weeks, Gregg opened up a little more and told me about his family. Gregg's parents had separated when he was twelve and he had gone to live with his father. He and his father had had to learn to take care of themselves. In fact, they had worked so hard at being self-sufficient that Gregg had forgotten what it was like to have someone take care of him. In one particular session, Gregg talked about the early years, before the divorce. With these memories came the feelings of loss; a tenderness and vulnerability surfaced in Gregg's personality. While he reexperienced these moments and allowed himself to feel the sadness that he previously had avoided, he found support in Lorelei's presence. As he stroked her gently, he talked to her about how much he missed his mother's warmth and love. He even allowed himself to cry. Role playing with Lorelei he recreated many of those nurturing moments of his childhood. Gregg's experience in childhood and his adult "indepedence" had caused him to avoid a satisfying love relationship because he would not allow himself to experience the feelings of vulnerability, trust, and mutual need. In the months ahead Gregg reestablished communication with his departed fiancée. They worked together on their new relationship. Gregg concentrated on making a deep commitment, and eventually the two were married.

A satisfying connection with a lover is more than a well-played tennis game or romantic weekend tryst. We must leave room for the care and attention that will encourage love to flourish. It takes time to develop trust in a stable relationship, especially if our parents separated or divorced in our early years. But with the help of a pet therapist, even deeply buried childhood disappointments can be resolved and a new foundation for love can be laid.

Both Marlene and Gregg used my pet therapists to help them rekindle their early loving experiences. Stroking a responsive pet therapist can bring you into immediate contact with what you are feeling. Experiencing yourself as a tender, vulnerable person is essential in accepting your need for love. Making this step allows you to acknowledge the softer parts of yourself, and prepares you to let a loving human relationship into your life.

Exercise Six: Accepting the Need for Love

You can use your own pet as a responsive therapist and experience the same supportive interaction that Marlene and Gregg had with my animals. Following is an exercise you can use at home to remember loving experiences with a parent and relive the joys of childish vulnerability.

1. Allow yourself some uninterrupted quiet time. Sit on the floor or on the couch with your pet.

2. Slowly stroke your animal. Take a few deep breaths.

3. Let yourself think back to the warm, loving feelings you had with one or both of your parents. Remember how special you felt and how much they cared about you. It may be a memory of being tucked into bed at night with a hug and a kiss. Or the feeling you had when you were given a push high in the air on your favorite swing. Maybe it was the first birthday or Christmas that you got the gift you wanted, and you saw the joy in your parents' eyes as you opened the package. You knew how much you were loved and how important you were to your parents.

4. Now let your mind go back to other caring moments. Continue to stroke your pet and feel its warmth. Close your eyes and stay with that feeling for a few minutes. When you open your eyes, you will still have that warm feeling inside you.

Your pet therapist has led you back to the images and feelings that nurtured your childhood. Some of these positive messages may have been forgotten in your attempts to become independent of your family. But now you are ready to integrate these vulnerable, tender parts of yourself with your mature adult. You have made contact with your own sense of caring.

You can repeat this exercise with your pet therapist whenever you need it. It will become easier as you practice it. You and your animal will create a readiness for you to accept the love that is available to you.

IDENTIFYING YOUR
FEAR OF INTIMACY

Everyone knows an attractive single person who always has a date but never falls in love. This is the agile single person who treats romantic partners as if they were opponents on a tennis court. This person is running on automatic and often has an unfinished battle with a parent. He or she is not seeing others as they actually are, but, instead is looking through a lens of distorted childhood memories. He or she is living out an unfinished dialogue with a parent in a self-destructive manner.

Living by an Outdated Script

One of my patients, Caroline, suffered from just this problem. At forty-four years of age and divorced, she was a successful businesswoman whose disappointments in love had caused her to be afraid of intimacy. Talent and persistence had combined to place her high in the executive office of a competitive advertising agency. Her accounts were prestigious and her creative campaigns assured her both financial success and recognition by her peers. Yet she was a consistent failure in romance; her career was working but her love life was not. Caroline came into therapy, discouraged and disgusted with her latest romance.

"I thought I had finally found the right man in Peter. With my son, Eric, leaving for college in the fall, I feel there is space in my life for another man at last. I don't think I want to get married again, but I would like to have someone to come home to at night. I have such a hectic schedule; I need someone to put his arms around me and bring me back to reality. Peter is bright and sensitive. It seemed to be working, but in the end he got competitive about my making so much money, and we ended up arguing over every little thing. It always happens that way with me. At the beginning of a relationship they see me as glamorous and indispensable. Then either I get bored, or they find my work too challenging for their egos. I'm afraid I'm going to end up old and alone."

Caroline began to cry as she recalled the bitter disappointments over her failures in love. Hearing her sobs Lorelei came over. Caroline reached down and stroked her head, crying even harder. It had been a long time since Caroline had let her real feelings surface. I knew she was ready now to look at her part of these unsuccessful relationships.

In the next sessions Caroline told me of her childhood and of her alcoholic father, whose changeable moods had caused him to swing back and forth from being an attentive, caring parent to being a critical, demanding ogre. Her mother had escaped the situation by starting her own design business, leaving Caroline at home to placate her bitter and troubled father. She let herself express the anger and helplessness that she had felt as a child, when she never knew in what mood she would find her father. She acted out some of these childhood scenes with Lorelei, pretending that Lorelei was her father. In these scenes Caroline finally let out her turbulent feelings about her difficult younger years. In the end she spoke softly to Lorelei of the sadness she felt that she had never been able to admit to her father.

Caroline had held these disappointments and feelings of anger within for many years. She had gone through the motions of creating a loving relationship, but without being aware of it, she always found a way to sabotage each romance. Through each one she had been living by an outdated script, seeing not a lover but her father. With the help of her pet therapist, she began to resolve her pain and lay aside her disappointment with her father.

The noncritical, loving pet can break through old messages and help us move on to fresh outlooks. The animal therapist will not fight on the family battlefield but instead will offer unconditional support and acceptance. More specifically, contact with your pet can help bring a hidden problem into focus. Role playing with your pet therapist by recalling angry, painful experiences can bring about a resolution of these old problems. Following is an exercise you can perform at home with your pet to work out unfinished scripts with your parents so you may start laying aside past angers and begin living without preconceptions.

Exercise Seven: Revising an Old Script

1. Find a quiet place and sit down with your pet. Close your eyes and take a few deep breaths.

2. Slowly touch your pet and let yourself imagine that your mother or father is sitting there with you.

3. *Now think about a particular disappointment you have felt — something you needed but didn't get, a painful incident for which you feel she or he was responsible. There may be something you have always wanted to say but have never had the courage to until now. Experience the supportive presence of your pet therapist.*

4. *Put into words what you have felt yet have never allowed yourself to say. As you stroke your pet, allow yourself to feel the anger or hurt. (If it is anger that you feel, you may need to turn away from your pet for a moment and let your fists clench and strike out.)*

5. *When you have expressed this memory in words and feelings, open your eyes and stroke your pet again.*

6. *Now imagine that your pet is the parent you have just encountered in your fantasy. Think what your parent would say if she or he could let you know her or his side of the story. Perhaps your need was never known or, because of your parent's own emotional difficulties she or he could not give you what you needed.*

7. *Now let yourself experience your disappointment again, and see if you can feel some difference inside yourself. Touch your animal therapist and feel its support and care. Ask yourself if you are ready to begin to forgive your parent for what you did not receive. Stroke your pet and let yourself feel some, even if incomplete, peaceful resolution of that old battle. You can begin to understand that you don't need to fight it anymore.*

This exercise may need to be repeated several times if the pain is deeply buried. Be patient with yourself. At another time you may have unfinished work with your other parent. Follow the same steps and let your feelings guide you to a resolution.

COUNTERACTING LONELINESS BY CONNECTING WITH OTHERS

Many single people of the baby boom generation complain that they find it difficult to meet people to date. Those who live in large cities, particularly new arrivals, find it especially difficult to make new friends. The bar scene and dating services can cause both sexes to feel like merchandise on display. In addition, recent demographics show that there are simply too few available men compared with the number of single women in the United States. No wonder singles complain of loneliness!

There is, of course, a difference between being alone and being lonely. There are occasions when we derive pleasure and contentment from having time to ourselves. We can put on our oldest clothes, make a cup of tea, curl up with a book, and have our cat or dog at our feet. There are other times, however, when we feel isolated and need company. We yearn for excitement, romance, a crazy evening with someone who appreciates us.

If this feeling hits us when we're stranded without a plan for the day, we may begin to feel desperate and sorry for ourselves. This feeling tends to spiral into inhibition ("If I'm alone, everyone will think I'm undesirable") and a further lowering of self-esteem ("I have nothing to say that anyone would be interested in hearing anyway"). At such times we can turn to our pet therapist for inspiration to help us break the loneliness barrier.

Using Your Pet to Break Through Loneliness

In my practice I see many single and divorced people who have successful careers but who feel baffled and discouraged at their failure to meet a romantic partner.

Elizabeth, a twenty-six-year-old film researcher, came to me because she had just such problems. When she first came to therapy, she described herself as painfully shy. She was a talented writer who found it easier to express her feelings on paper. She was lonely and came into therapy to work out her inhibitions about forming relationships. "I think I hide behind my books and writing. It's less risky and I feel embarrassed when I'm with a group. I know I must scare off men with my stiffness. If only I could get myself to relax and encourage them!"

I soon learned that Elizabeth had grown up as an only child. As a result she had spent more time reading books than playing with other children. One of her favorite pastimes had been to play theater games with her English cocker spaniel, Veronica. In these games the two of them would act out many of the characters in literature and history. Veronica would enthusiastically play queen to Elizabeth's Prince Albert or Romeo to a tragic Juliet. Romantic fantasy had been a part of Elizabeth's childhood. During the beginning months of her therapy, she came to understand the need to accept reality. During her second year in therapy, she began to develop the right balance between fantasy and reality. In addition, she developed the inner strength to let herself admit the need for a real relationship. Then she became ready to risk, and to practice some skills in, connecting with men.

Lars was another patient who had no problems achieving his career goals, yet needed help in achieving personal goals. Most of all, he needed to develop confidence in his ability to meet women. At twenty-eight he had come to the United States from Norway to do graduate work in business administration at a major university. He was intelligent and handsome, but afraid to face the women in his new country. "I didn't know where to start. At home I had many female friends. I didn't have to worry. But American women are different. I don't know how to make a good impression."

Lars was too hard on himself. He expected far too much of himself in social situations and consequently appeared quite self-conscious. I decided to introduce Lars to my pet therapist. I suggested he role play with Lorelei to practice his approach to women. Because Lars was so nervous about saying the wrong thing to someone new, I had him intentionally exaggerate his dialogue by introducing himself in every crazy, embarrassing way conceivable. Playing with Lorelei, who responded favorably to everything he said and in a sense became a romantic mime, gave Lars a chance to relax and to put his attempts to make conversation into perspective. With a little guidance from me, along with Lorelei's undemanding and responsive support and some honest self-appraisal, Lars learned to be more self-accepting and less critical. But even with these great steps forward, he still had trouble meeting new people.

With the help of therapy, Elizabeth and Lars had learned to feel better about themselves. They had gained some much-needed self-confidence and self-esteem. But they still needed to practice their skills in meeting people. I introduced the "Petcology Date Finder," an exercise consisting of a number of steps designed to sharpen these skills, with nearly immediate results.

Elizabeth purchased a golden retriever puppy and took her to obedience school. Drawing on her newly discovered self-possession she sought out an owner who attracted her, and without giving a thought to her previously inhibiting shyness, she introduced herself. During the course she began dating him. The last I heard, both man and dog had moved in. Lars was unable to keep a pet, so he borrowed Lorelei for regular Sunday walks on the univeristy campus, keeping in mind that he needed to practice his social skills. At first the walks took less than thirty minutes. He had trouble with this exercise until I reminded him to relax, exude confidence, and be more approachable. Slowly, the times of his walks lengthened. And, after one such outing, he came back reporting happily that he had made a date for the next week with a woman he'd just met.

A dog has a quality that invites people to approach. Even some cats can be trained to walk on a leash — and a cat on a leash is a real traffic stopper. People walking their dogs or cats seem friendly and safe, and shy people are more self-assured in the company of their pet therapists.

Exercise Eight: The Petcology Date Finder

1. When walking your dog, allow it to lead you to someone you find attractive. If someone approaches you don't frown or show impatience. Instead, recognize this friendly intrusion as an opportunity to get to know someone new.

2. Start a routine walk in a park. If you don't own a pet, notice those who do. Stop and admire one or two. Ask questions about the pet. Be certain to remember the pet's name. The next time you see the pet and owner together, be sure to greet them both. Don't forget to smile at the animal. (They have a good memory for smiles.)

3. At art fairs, shopping malls, or swap meets, be sure to bring your canine along. Quite likely, someone will stop to talk to you.

4. Watch the local papers for dog or cat shows. Try to attend one and look for someone who is alone with his or her pet. Discuss his or her animal and ask permission to take a photograph. Get the person's telephone number so that you can call when the picture is developed.

5. Consider buying a dog. If you do buy one, take a dog obedience class. Find the owner who most interests you. Then be sure to ask lots of questions about his or her pet. (Talk about your animals' breeding or success with the obedience class.)

6. If you absolutely cannot own a pet, don't worry! Just make it a point to drop in to your local pet store or animal shelter on a regular basis; animal lovers abound at these places!

Activities such as those in the Date Finder are an easy and amusing way to practice connection skills. These small steps help you develop poise. Soon it all seems very natural, and it's only a matter of time before you devise your own methods for meeting others and let yourself be swept into a satisfying relationship.

FINDING THE RIGHT MATE

Making the right choices, avoiding the hurtful dating game, and surviving rejection all challenge the unattached person in search of a permanent relationship. All of us have a natural need to love: we want to have someone to come home to after a fast-paced day at work; we want to share our pleasures and our problems with that special someone. Weekends and holidays are more fun knowing we will be with the person we love. But many unattached people do not get beyond that first exciting, hopeful date. What's the secret to moving past the dreamy beginning and on to something that lasts?

Don't Rely on Shortcuts
When Looking for Your Mate

Unfortunately, there are pitfalls on the road from date to mate. For many singles a strong sense of self-worth is lacking. Becoming attracted to the wrong person and spending years with an interesting but emotionally unavailable lover is another familiar story. Many fear rejection and have painful memories of past romantic failures. They may also have lingering doubts about their own lovability or sexual adequacy. These feelings of vulnerability and fear of loss often push singles into trying to outguess their dates' desires instead of relating to them in a natural way.

Singles often fantasize of instant love, but a fast leap into togetherness just doesn't work. In addition, they may fall into a different, but equally dangerous, fantasy that as lovers they are very much alike. If people are afraid of being known as they are, they will ignore their unique contributions to the relationship; they will never dare to be different!

Developing a relationship requires time and persistence. There are no shortcuts! It takes patience to explore and test the ground you and your new love share. You can and should learn from past mistakes and unfortunate choices. And with work, it is possible to avoid the fantasy of instant love and to differentiate between the excitement of a new love and the actual person you will come to love. But succeeding in this requires self-knowledge and attention to your own needs. In other words, you must have confidence in the "I" before you can trust the "we."

Searching for the right relationship is a natural part of single life. Unfortunately, we must live through a number of wrong relationships to find the right one. And if our needs are hidden and our ability to see another in a realistic light is impaired, we go from one relationship to the next seeking an ideal that does not exist. Many people have the inclination to choose exactly the wrong person. We may look for someone who is exciting and challenging when our actual need is for someone who is giving, stable, and willing to commit to a relationship. On the other hand, we may remain with a partner who is safe and secure but with whom we cannot grow. I have worked with many people who fell in love with a fantasized ideal and when the reality emerged, pain and disappointment were the result.

Stop and Evaluate Yourself
and Your Past Relationships

Pets can be a source of support while you're evaluating your choice for a mate and working at strengthening this love relationship. Once you've met your new love, your pet will help when you and your lover undergo those tests that every new couple must pass. For instance, while you wait for your telephone to ring, you may begin to doubt your lovability; you can turn to your pet therapist in order to clarify your needs and goals. Your pet therapsit will be there, too, if the relationship falls apart. The animal's love for you will be a constant reminder of your value.

Nancy was a woman who had not yet found a permanent love relationship and was having trouble doing so. Over the years she had used her artistic talent to develop a dress designing business. This work satisfied her creative and financial needs, but as a result, any outside interests were given low priority, including dating. Her hectic schedule included diplomatically handling customers, settling the daily business accounts, and making trips to fashion centers in other cities. Her most recent relationship had ended a year ago. Nancy enjoyed her work but she missed having a steady relationship. She also was worried about turning forty. Nancy decided to come into therapy.

"I'm afraid I've forgotten how to date," Nancy said, checking to make sure that her blouse was neatly tucked into her business-like suit. Her hair was perfect, her nails nicely manicured, and her makeup just right. "I spent three years with a married man, believing he was going to get a divorce. Finally, I realized he never would. That was a year ago. It was so easy when I was younger; there was always some man around who appealed to me. Then, when I started concentrating on building up my business, my focus shifted: I thought only about work. I've had plenty of boyfriends, but I've always seemed to take them for granted and I've eventually lost them. Most of them have gone on to marry someone else. Now I definitely want to settle down. But what should I do? Where should I start?"

Nancy began by looking at her series of nonproductive and self-defeating relationships. In the past ten years, in each instance, she had chosen dynamic and successful men. But none of them had wanted to marry her. She had hidden beneath her business-like exterior; she had played with them and challenged them, but she had never allowed the serious or tender sides of her personality to show. Nancy had treated love as a pastime.

We looked at the pattern of her parents' marriage. We saw particularly that Nancy's mother had never been happy in her marriage; she had wanted her daughter to avoid a similar pitfall. As a result, Nancy's family, most especially her mother, had praised her independent, competitive spirit but ignored her softer, more vulnerable qualities. They had taught her to be financially independent but had forgotten to encourage her to lead a stable life, with a husband and children.

While Nancy reevaluated her old relationships, she found a lovable and accepting listener in my pet therapist Clancy. Nancy threw off her shoes and curled up on the couch and stroked his fur. She shed her businesslike veneer and exhibited feelings of tenderness and vulnerability. She went through many difficult emotions as she recalled past mistakes of her love life. Through it all Clancy was always there with an encouraging purr or nudge. Nancy decided to purchase a long-haired Persian, whom she called Salome. She had long conversations at home with Salome about her need for love. As a result of our sessions and her conversations with Salome, Nancy became aware that she had a side to her that was not at all business, that she indeed was capable of vulnerability. She also realized that she was her own woman, and she did not have to carry out her mother's desires or repeat her mistakes. In addition, she realized that as a defense against failure with men, she had learned to put work ahead of love. When she learned to separate her own needs from those of her mother and to reassess how she had been choosing her lovers, she then established a more satisfying love relationship.

Realize Your Individuality

Don, thirty-four, was another patient who was depressed and discouraged about his ability to find lasting love, but his failures in love had come because he had refused to show his lovers that he could be independent. He came to me right after his second wife had left him. Both of his wives had been outgoing, intelligent, successful women. The marriages had started out fine, but then each had deteriorated into disastrous bickering. Eventually, both women had left him. Don's problem was that he had deceived himself into believing he could live his life through his wives' challenges and not bother to find his own way. He had been attracted by their assertiveness, but their strong personalities had only increased his tendency to be dependent and passive.

"I don't know what I want in a woman. I think I need some time to see what I'm about. Whenever I would find a woman I liked I would jump into a serious relationship right away. I would become so dependent on them: I was always worrying about what they wanted, what kind of mood they were in, and how I may have upset them. I thought if I could understand them, they would take care of my needs. I've spent too much time trying to guess their moods. I guess this behavior worked in getting attention from my mother."

I learned that Don had married right out of college. He had therefore avoided learning about himself, and he had never known how to make the right choice in love. I had him work with Delilah, describing and acting out some of his past efforts to please both his mother and his ex-wives. There were moments of anger and there was even some laughter as he pantomimed around Delilah; he concentrated on his past and was able to put his feelings into perspective. He became more aware of his own needs. He began to date different women and found he needed work in discriminating between what he wanted and what they wanted. With Delilah's support, Don learned to realize his own individuality; he came to appreciate his work as a teacher, his hobbies, and his values. Since the beginning of Don's dating days, he had never understood himself or the women with whom he had become involved. He had seen them only through the haze of what he had thought were his inner needs. When the women had not responded to those needs, he had behaved in a helpless way, appealing to their maternal qualities. He had fooled himself into thinking he was less capable than these women, and he had always measured himself against what he had thought were their superior qualities. As a result he had lost his own sense of individuality as well as the women whom he had loved. Fortunately, Don realized that with therapy and with support from his pet therapist, he could change his perceptions and his love patterns. He continued to date on a casual basis while learning about himself and appreciating his women friends for who they actually were.

Recognize Self-Defeating Patterns

There are those who consistently select the wrong person as a mate. These people often are in love with the idea of love, and have an impossibly idealistic image of the perfect mate. This occurs most commonly as a result of childhood patterns or even one incident in childhood. Inevitably, the search for the perfect mate winds up in failure. These self-defeating patterns must be recognized and curbed, and realistic expectations must be adopted. The Relationship Inventory (see Exercise Nine) helps to break negative relationship patterns.

Exercise Nine: The Relationship Inventory

In my practice I see that the one who initiates the breakup and the one who is left feel equally disturbed by the experience. If you are the one who has decided to leave, you may feel responsible, guilty, and frightened about the future. You may also worry that you have made the wrong decision. If you are the one who has been left, you may feel betrayed, abandoned, and unlovable. When a relationship ends you can let yourself go into a tailspin and blame yourself, or you can use that time to evaluate your love history. Use the Relationship Inventory to assess the pattern of your romantic choices and to review your responsibility for what took place between you and your lovers. You may find that you have unrealistic hopes. You can use your pet therapist as a supportive listener to help you discover your patterns and begin to understand what is going on in your life. The Relationship Inventory will give you a new orientation and help you gain control over your future choices. This exercise can work with or without the presence of an animal, but progress in self-understanding generally is faster with one. Naturally, your pet is not the only one who can listen to you. Friends or family can offer support too. But your pet is always there, won't give you inappropriate advice, never judges you, and is always loving.

1. Curl up with your pet, and make a list of all the relationships you have had over the past few years. Under each name write down what attracted you to that person. What were your major needs in the relationship, and how did you communicate them to your partner? Were there any common threads among the people you selected? What bothered you the most? What made it go sour? What were you seeking? Did you believe that his or her success, assurance, ambition, or determination would transfer to you through proximity?

2. Choose the relationship that at this time carries the strongest emotional content for you. Strong emotions indicate that you are holding some unspoken words and feelings inside. Imagine that your pet therapist is that old love to whom you still feel tied. Take a few deep breaths and express your resentments about what took place. State out loud some of the hopes and frustrations you may not have expressed during the relationship.

3. Imagine the answer your ex-lover would give. How does it make you feel? You may experience a welling up of sadness as you encounter your old romantic dream. You may realize you simply projected your hopes onto your lover, never really knowing him or her. You may start with a fury of disappointment and end up realizing it was an impossible expectation from the beginning. Are there other things you need to say to feel more finished?

Take as much time as you need. You may find that you want to let that person know what your resonsibility was in what took place between you.

4. *When you feel ready try saying a symbolic good-bye to your old love. This may just be the start of a farewell; you may need to repeat this exercise again with your pet.*

5. *Now give your pet a hug and yourself some praise for your courage and honesty. Look at your inventory and see if you need to repeat this exercise with another old love.*

You can do this with any unfinished relationship. You will find that you begin to lose the unrealistic fantasies you had been carrying from one love to the next. It's much easier to face our unrealistic dreams and to look at our responsibilities with a supportive pet therapist by our side.

UNDERSTANDING THE PLEASURES AND FEARS OF COMMITMENT

For most people the purpose of dating is to find a suitable lifetime partner. As a dating relationship evolves, therefore, myriad questions arise about one's readiness to commit to a live-in relationship or marriage. In fact, my experience shows that one major reason people enter therapy is to decide if they are ready for a permanent relationship. How do you know whether you care enough for a person to make the commitment? What tells you that you are ready to give up some personal space and some independence to live together? Couples contemplating a permanent relationship often fear becoming too dependent and losing individuality.

Sharing with someone else requires working out your own feelings of self-worth and individuality. You can't share part of what you have if you believe you don't have enough. You need the confidence that you will be able to maintain your boundaries and sense of self-worth. You need to trust that you will know what you need and will not expect your mate to know that for you. Your first responsibility will be to maintain your own sense of worth and integrity. If your self-esteem is shaky, you might worry about being swallowed up by your mate's opinions, feelings, and way of life. You need to trust yourself before you can trust someone you love enough to consider living with or marrying him or her.

How Do You Deal With Your Differences?

Two people who contemplate living together face numerous differences in background and experience. Couples can potentially disagree about sex, money, in-laws, work, leisure time, housework, children, goals, and even pets — for starters. The ability to respect differences and talk openly can determine whether a relationship will grow or flounder. It is not the disagreements that are important but how we deal with them.

Jon, a patient of mine, hesitated to marry because he was afraid to deal with the differences between himself and his girlfriend. Thus he could not decide *how* to take the final step into marriage, which nearly destroyed the relationship altogether. Jon, forty-six and divorced once, owned a restaurant. He put a high premium on seeing his male friends for a weekly poker game and going on fishing trips with them. During his marriage he had put aside these interests and forced himself to work unbelievably long hours, enrolling his children in private schools and subsidizing his wife's music studio. He had been brought up to believe that putting your wife and children first was crucial to being a good husband. Jon had not learned to find a place for himself in that marriage. After his divorce he became involved with Jeri, thirty-two, an intriguing model. She was not as enthusiastic about sports as he was, but his attachment to her had overcome most of his doubts. Still, considering his last marital failure, he worried about the ultimate step of this relationship — marriage.

"What if we get married and it all goes sour? What if I get locked into her needs and forget my own? We have an exciting relationship now, but I don't want to lose my new sense of independence. What will she do if I want to go hunting for a week and she doesn't want me to go?"

From our discussions I knew that Jon was in love. But was he ready for marriage? During the following weeks he talked about his fear of expressing his needs in a relationship and his belief that love could not contain his and Jeri's separate interests. I asked him to take a close look at what he wanted to share with her and what they could allow each other in separateness. I suggested he take the Commitment Readiness Quiz, which follows. His score showed that he and his Old English sheepdog, Molesworth, were ready to live with Jeri.

Feeling Trapped

Sometimes the idea of making a commitment brings back past feelings of helplessness, when one partner felt trapped by the pressure of commitment. If these feelings surface, then hesitancy prevails. Before a new commitment can be made, the person must resolve the unfinished painful experiences in order to understand them and how they have been suppressed. Role playing with one's pet therapist (see Exercise Seven: Revising an Old Script) can help to resolve these problems.

Exercise Ten: Commitment Readiness Quiz

When the final step toward making a permanent commitment is taken, couples often find themselves struggling with traces of unfinished relationships. The wounds of previous alliances must be healed and resolved before the new couple is free to commit to each other. Examining your present level of trust and interest in sharing your life can predict some of the pleasures or problems of the future. The Commitment Readiness Quiz is one way to measure a couple's ability to establish a permanent relationship. It helps to evaluate if you are ready for a lifetime together by looking at your attitude toward your lover's relationship with your pet. Are you willing to share pleasures and responsibilities and work out the differences? This test is one measure of your readiness to open your life to someone you love.

Circle the number that best fits what you feel about each question:

AGREE   DISAGREE
5   4   3   2   1

1. I would let my pet get its bone or catnip from him or her instead of from me. 5   4   3   2   1

2. I would let my pet sleep on his or her side of the bed.   5   4   3   2   1

3. I would try his or her way of obedience training even if if were different from mine. 5   4   3   2   1

4. If someone admired my pet on a walk, I would let him or her take the praise. 5   4   3   2   1

5. *If we went on vacation, I would be open to his or her opinion about what to do with my pet.*   5   4   3   2   1

6. *If my pet won a prize at a show, I would let him or her pick up the blue ribbon.*   5   4   3   2   1

7. *If my pet were destructive to our home, I would consider my mate's way of discipline even if it were not in sync with mine.*   5   4   3   2   1

8. *If we disagreed on birth control or breeding for my pet, I would be open to his or her opinion.*   5   4   3   2   1

9. *If my pet got sick, I would listen to his or her opinion on veterinary treatment.*   5   4   3   2   1

10. *If he or she wanted to add another pet to our household, I would consider it.*   5   4   3   2   1

Now total your score. What does your score mean?

50–42 points: You are now ready for the big step! You appear to be confident in your sense of individuality and feel that you can share your life and your pet without losing what is important to you.

41–32 points: You need to talk about it some more. There are still some unresolved issues for you, but you are close to feeling secure in taking the next step. Review with your lover some of these doubts about asserting your needs and how you can work these out.

31 points or less: You'd better reevaluate. Either you're with the wrong person, or you have too many unresolved issues of your own. Stop and evaluate what you want in your life and how you have been going about getting it. Sit down with your pet therapist and review the exercises in this chapter. Plan what you can do to make the best assessment of your needs and what you will do to make the right decision this time.

The Commitment Readiness Quiz can also serve as a way to promote honest discussion about fears and differences, because the quiz measures your openness to making a serious commitment. After all, sharing your space, your friends, and especially your pet will be part of the adjustment of living together. If two people are able to communicate their disagreements and respect each other's attitudes, they can build a solid foundation for working out the normal conflicts they will face in living together or in marriage.

SUMMARY

People often shy away from closeness, because they fear a loss of independence and individuality. Competitive work roles and fast-paced activities can disguise our vulnerability and need for love. Unresolved battles with a parent may hold a person in a self-defeating script that does not allow for intimacy. Singles and newly divorced people struggle with loneliness and search for ways to make connections with the opposite sex. Surviving the dating scene and developing a lasting relationship often requires a reevaluation of love choices and reassessment of relationship patterns.

Our animals can help us through each step on the path to building a satisfying love relationship. They can help us recognize the need for closeness and give us support to open ourselves to that experience. They can help lead us to that all-important love connection and encourage a sense of ease as we develop intimacy. We can use them to explore our readiness for a permanent commitment. Through their presence and acceptance they can teach us how to develop the foundation for a lasting relationship.

Next we look at how our pet therapists can help us develop open communcation and trust as we try to resolve the conflicts that inevitably arise in marriage.

CHAPTER FOUR

Resolving Conflict With Your Partner

M arriage (or, for some, a permanent live-in relationship) is once again in fashion. Today 90 percent of all American men and women marry at least once. Six out of seven of those who divorce remarry within three years. But many changes have taken place in marriage. Men and women, who today have ever more education and leisure time, enter marriage with higher expectations but with less time to give their relationship. The current career orientation of women often puts pressure on both wives and husbands. Tensions develop over money, time, domestic roles, jealousy, sex, and the all-important question of whether to have children.

The relationship between women and men has come a long way since Penelope patiently waited ten years for Odysseus to return from his adventures in Troy. But the dream of having a unique relationship that lasts a lifetime has not changed since the ancient Greeks. Psychologist Carl Rogers in *Becoming Partners: Marriage and Its Alternatives* (N.Y.: Dell Publishing, 1972) talks of the complexities of present man–woman relationships. He believes that, despite the increasing emotional demands that couples face, there is hope for an enriched permanence in marriage. Certainly, making a bond that will last and will allow for individual growth within the relationship is no easy task. People whose marriages survive need flexibility, commitment, humor, and the ability to relax and enjoy each other.

Today the majority of women work before and during marriage. Many couples whom I counsel laughingly tell me that what they both need is an old-fashioned wife. A pet can offer emotional support to both partners. When the front door is opened, a warm, eager, enthusiastic pet will run to greet the person, offering instant gratification and abundant love. Let's see how pets can help busy couples reduce tensions and solve problems.

THE ROAD FROM DREAM TO REALITY

During dating, couples often focus most on what they have in common. They delight in finding similar tastes in movies, restaurants, books, and travel. They often dress and act to please each other. Projecting a romantic ideal onto their future mates, they close their eyes to differences in values and expectations. But after marriage people find that living together can bring out conflicts that were pushed under the rug during courtship. A tug-of-war begins. Can two people maintain individuality and growth and still preserve their love?

COMMUNICATION IS THE KEY

Often a couple is not aware of how they fall into patterns and have false expectations. Trying to second guess a partner's needs is a destructive habit. The two people then become disappointed with each other's performances, and they fall into the habit of blaming each other and trying to prove who is right. Defining and communicating needs in a more positive way is the first step toward resolving conflicts.

Ron and Melanie illustrate a typical pattern of miscommunication in marriage. They had been married one year when they came to me for help because of their increasing arguments. Melanie, twenty-nine, was a nurse, and Ron, thirty-two, had been attracted to her warm, nurturing sensitivity. Ron was climbing the corporate ladder in the computer industry, and expected Melanie to "be there" when he needed her. During their courtship Melanie had longed for the role of a supportive wife and had encouraged him to depend on her. She came from a military family that was always on the go, and she had dreamed of a stable home life with Ron. But after a year of marriage, she had become restless and distant, feeling trapped by Ron's need for her. What she had previously considered romantic intimacy now felt like a suffocating demand for constant attention.

She talked to me as Ron waited impatiently for an opportunity to interrupt her. "I feel like I'm a mother, not a wife. I work too, but Ron takes it for granted that I'll be the shopper and the cook. I thought having a husband and a home would help me feel loved and secure. But I spend most of my time listening to his complaints about company hassles and trying to keep his spirits up. I look after patients all day, and when I come home I have to look after him too. Who takes care of me?"

Ron was hurt and angry. "You were the one who wanted to get married in such a big hurry. You knew that my career would depend on my performance during the next few years. A year ago you were excited about cooking exotic foreign dishes. Now I feel like I'm living with a martyr instead of a wife. This is the kind of fighting we do at home and I'm sick of it."

I could see instantly that theirs was a battle going nowhere. They had become expert blamers and had forgotten how to listen to each other. They both thought they were right in every argument and would not back down. I asked them to describe a recent incident in which they had disagreed. Interestingly enough, their disagreement was about adopting a neighborhood cat. Ron wanted to take the orphan in and, although Melanie liked the kitten, she already felt overwhelmed with household responsibilities. "I'll end up taking full care of the cat," Melanie said, "and you know I'm right." I asked both of them to express their feelings and then to state what responsibilities they would be willing to undertake. Ron agreed to feed the cat and take it to the veterinarian. Melanie was surprised at Ron's offer. She agreed to purchase the cat food and groom it. They would each take turns with the litter box. From this discussion Melanie saw that if she was clear about what she was and was not willing to do, Ron would listen to her. She was not obligated to accept full responsibility and then feel resentful. In fact, she found that Ron was willing to be helpful when he understood exactly what she wanted from him.

Couples do not usually deliberately deceive each other about their expectations for marriage, but they do often overestimate their capabilities. For Ron and Melanie, solving the problem of adopting the cat showed them that success was possible with an issue that was not argued to death. At their next appointment they told me that they had adopted the cat and were sharing the responsibilities. Using this easily remedied problem as a beginning, we then turned to some of the more emotional issues of their relationship: taking care of the home, being available to listen, and making love. Being a good partner meant different things to each of them. Once they looked at their notions about marriage and modified them to meet each other's needs, they stopped blaming each other, learned to solve problems, and began to enjoy their marriage.

Learn to be Open with your Spouse

Mark and Sherry's problems are typical of those experienced by two-career couples who expect marriage to automatically provide them with emotional support. Mark, thirty-six, and Sherry, thirty, had married after two tumultuous years of dating and breaking up. They had finally agreed to marry. Sherry had felt a permanent commitment was what she needed; Mark had found Sherry exciting and had believed that he had found the perfect partner. While Mark struggled to acquire new clients for his editing business, Sherry was successful as head of an accounting firm. Eight months after they married, they found themselves filled with unresolved resentments. At my office their faces were strained with tension.

"Mark is critical and never satisfied with me. He reminds me of my mother, who was also impossible to please. The house is never neat enough and dinner is never just right. Weekends are filled with work that he has stacked up to be done. Before we got married we had fun. Now it's just work and arguing." Sherry continued to describe her dissatisfactions in a cool, logical manner, which reflected her training in accounting.

Unfortunately, Sherry's objectivity inspired Mark to argumentative vigor. He started off with, "You're wrong! I'm not critical. I'm just sick of coming home late and finding you curled up with work. I need a warm, loving woman, not a financial expert. You're always thinking of something else, and you're never turned on when I want to make love. I come home totally exhausted to a cluttered house, and you're sitting there preparing work for someone else. You never have time for me." Mark reached down to pet Lorelei, whose presence seemed to calm his anger.

This dialogue was the beginning of several months of serious therapy for them. I stressed to them that marriage can serve as a source of warmth and security for both partners, but it takes sensitivity and an openness to self-understanding to make the partnership work.

During our next sessions I learned that Sherry's parents had divorced when she was twelve. Her mother had been more interested in a business career than in motherhood. Unconsciously, she had given Sherry a model for career success without thinking about her daughter's need for intimacy. Sherry's training in accounting had further added to her tendency to value order. As a result Sherry paid little attention to her softer, more vulnerable side. She felt more comfortable solving business problems than dealing with emotions.

The first thing to do was to start a dialogue between Mark and Sherry. Lorelei and I served as intermediaries. Slowly, they learned to be more open with each other. Sherry shared some feelings of inadequacy about her femininity. She also said that she was afraid to let herself act unreasonable or out of control. As Sherry began to show a vulnerable side, Mark eased up and began to listen to his wife and understand her feelings.

Mark, on the other hand, learned that when he came home tired and emotionally depleted, he would become dissatisfied, critical, and demanding of his wife. He learned that he needed to set limits on his own work load so that he wouldn't come home so exhausted. As he tried out a new work schedule, he found he was not as demanding of himself or of Sherry. They both saw that they needed to take more responsibility for making plans to relax and enjoy each other again.

I had them practice listening to each other at home by using their cat, Miranda. They would set aside free time after dinner and curl up on the couch with Miranda. While stroking the cat, they would perform an exercise in empathetic listening. Mark would tell Sherry how he felt about an issue, and she would tell him what she thought he meant. Miranda's relaxing presence, along with their newfound patience, helped their relationship grow stronger.

Stroking Miranda encouraged them to exhibit quieter, softer qualities, thus teaching each to be both more self-accepting and more appreciative of the other. They also discovered that they didn't always have to be right.

A warm, accepting pet can be a helpful presence in an unproductive argument. The animal does not take sides. It doesn't care who is right or wrong, require explanations, or offer advice. Pets provide love instead of criticism. They listen and believe that both people can be "right." They offer support and respect each individual within the relationship.

Listening Breaks the Stalemate

Many factors can lead to poor communication between partners. Disappointment, hurt, and withdrawal are the ones that most often create a barrier to communication. Therapists and pets can offer emotional support as couples risk being vulnerable and open to each other. It takes patience to maintain intimacy within marriage, but the results are well worth the effort.

When Pam, twenty-nine, and Bob, thirty-five, married, Pam thought she had found a lover as well as the perfect father for Ken, her child from a previous marriage. Marrying Bob would provide her with the stability she had missed during her childhood years, which had been spent with an unpredictable, alcoholic father. Bob, an engineering executive, was conservative, even-tempered, and attracted to Pam's outgoing, fun-loving warmth. He had no children from his previous marriage and was looking forward to helping Pam raise her ten-year-old son. Neither could have predicted the disappointment and problems that would build up in their first two years of marriage. Pam barely entered my office before letting out her stored-up resentments.

"You hide your feelings and withdraw when we have a fight," she said as she faced her husband. "I am sick of having to approach every problem your way. I need to express my feelings, but I can't do it your way. You always act like such an expert. I feel stifled by your methods." I pointed out to Pam that if she needed Bob to be emotionally available to her, she would have to allow for their individual differences.

Bob reached down and gave my dog Delilah a pat. I could see that he was bracing himself for another barrage of criticism, and that he was trying to protect himself by freezing his emotional response to her anger. When Bob got frightened he retreated and tried to analyze what was going on between them. And when Bob withdrew and became emotionally unavailable, it brought back painful memories to Pam of her unpredictable, withdrawing father.

To break their destructive patterns of communication, I suggested they try a listening exercise. Using Delilah to help them, I asked that they put aside any logical arguments pertinent to the topic and instead just listen with an open heart and mind. Even if one did not agree with what the other said, the spouse should be listened to and be given ample time to be fully understood. Delilah sat nearby and could be patted and stroked; her presence might encourage Pam and Bob to be patient as they listened to each other.

I had Bob begin by telling Pam some of his needs. Bob talked about feeling inadequate in their relationship and described how frightened he was when he realized he was not always included in Pam's relationship with her son, Ken. He admitted hiding behind the role of expert, because it was familiar and safe. Pam sat quietly, stroking Delilah and listening until Bob was completely finished. When her turn came she told Bob how his reserve reminded her of her father. It became clear to Bob that her father's withdrawal had caused Pam to be afraid of intimacy. For once they stopped accusing and began listening to each other's need for love.

Following is a step-by-step exercise that uses your pet to help you improve your skills in listening to your mate, while remaining open and nondefensive. It requires practice not to answer back when you don't agree or when you feel accused of some deficiency. But wholehearted listening will nurture and strengthen your marriage.

Exercise Eleven: Listening to Your Lover

PART ONE: CLARIFYING YOUR NEED

1. Sit with your pet in a quiet place. Stroke the animal, take a few breaths, and relax.

2. Tell your pet about an important need of yours of which you believe your partner is unaware or does not fully understand. As you express this need out loud to your pet, listen carefully to what you are saying, for example, "Why can't he ever make dinner?" Is this really what you want your mate to hear? If it doesn't sound right, restate it in a different manner, for example, "I need him to help me get dinner ready when I get overloaded." Clarifying your need may take some patience, but your pet has plenty of time.

3. *When you feel satisfied that you are clear about your need, you are ready to talk to your lover.*

PART TWO: COMMUNICATING
WITH YOUR PARTNER

1. *Sit with your mate and your pet counselor.*

2. *Express the need to your partner that you have just rehearsed with your pet. Your mate should listen but not respond. (Your partner may not agree with you, but this is not the time to interrupt.)*

3. *When you have finished speaking, your mate will repeat what was said, in his or her own words.*

4. *If this message isn't what you intended to communicate, restate your need. Your partner should again refrain from responding.*

5. *Now your mate must repeat what was heard.*

6. *When you feel that your point has been fully understood, switch places with your partner. Start again with Part One: Clarifying Your Need, only this time it's your partner's turn to clarify a need to your pet therapist. Then come together and repeat Part Two: Communicating With Your Partner, during which you listen and repeat what you understood your partner to have said.*

When you have both had the opportunity to share your needs, allow yourselves a few minutes of silence together, just the two of you.

This exercise may be repeated whenever one of the partners feels it is necessary. If either of you feels tense or anxious during this exercise, take a few breaths and quietly stroke your pet. Your pet's serenity will help you remain open to this new form of communicating. Do not attempt it during an argument or before you have had the opportunity to think things through alone with your pet. Separating your thoughts and feelings is essential for clarification of the issue. This can hardly be done during heated conflict. If performed properly, this exercise will teach you to communicate effectively.

ROOM FOR TWO . . . TAKING A TENSION BREAK

Couples need emotional space. It is simply not necessary to make an issue of every annoyance that arises; not every resentment requires discussion. For couples who are married or live together, a breather from chronic irritations that occur in close relationships is vital.

Pets help create diversions from daily pressures and allow couples to gain perspective on conflicts. If a problem is serious, making an impulsive, angry statement to prove your case will not necessarily solve it. Allow your pet to help you relax. Take your pet aside and groom it, or go for a walk to cool off. This will give you a fresh approach to the problem. Your sense of humor may even return!

If you fall into a pattern of bickering, you may not see a way out of this destructive behavior. Your animal is the ideal distraction. Watching your cat chase its tail or having your dog bring a treasured bone to you can remind you of life's lighter side. When you return to your problem, you may find that it wasn't that bad. Some problems dissipate without intervention. But if you decide that an issue needs attention, a break from it will allow you to return with a new outlook. In addition, turning to a supportive pet can help you to clarify your needs and resolve conflict in a constructive way.

Finding the Right Time To Communicate

Another problem that couples often face is deciding on *when* to communicate; two people don't always want to talk or listen at the same time. For example, every evening Donna, thirty-four, and Rob, thirty-three, had the same disagreement. It would start like this: he would come home hungry and immediately join her in the kitchen, tasting the food or making unwanted contributions to her preparations. She didn't like him in the kitchen when she made dinner. No matter how often she told him this, Rob wouldn't cooperate. He wanted someone to talk to when he came home.

Donna preferred to get the news of his day during dinner. Predictably, this routine disagreement started the evening off badly.

It was obvious to me that Rob needed contact when he got home. Conversely, Donna needed quiet time, which she found in the kitchen preparing dinner. I suggested a way to break this unproductive habit. Rob had told me that he enjoyed playing outside with their Akita dog, Hari. I suggested he use this time to engage Hari in activity. This way Rob had the contact he needed, and Donna had the quiet time she coveted. Hari's presence helped both of them solve their needs.

Finding the right time to communicate effectively can create difficulties among partners. But the presence of a pet can ease this problem. Exercising or grooming the dog or taking the cat aside for some loving strokes are ways to respect the other's emotional privacy. Ignoring the need for space can cause minor differences to escalate into hurtful arguments. It is much more fun to play with your pet than to nitpick over small issues with your spouse.

APPRECIATING INDIVIDUAL DIFFERENCES

Different interests and minor disagreements are natural to couples. Two people may believe — mistakenly — that getting along requires the same viewpoint on all issues. But allowing room for differences is healthy and brings excitement to a marriage. Dealing with dissimilarities breaks up static patterns that can cultivate boredom. If looked upon positively, these differences can add richness to a relationship.

Don't Let Differences Interfere

Sometimes couples let differences get in the way of their marriage. Denny, twenty-seven, and Joan, twenty-five, had been married for a year and often got stuck on the same conflict — his parents. Denny, an only child, was used to keeping in close contact with his mother and father. Joan had left her family at an early age and had established her independence before getting married. It did not bother Denny that his parents called frequently and that they liked to visit unexpectedly, but Joan found it intrusive. Joan told me that

Denny was a pushover when it came to his mother; Denny contended that Joan was cold and wouldn't understand his close relationship with his parents. When I talked to them, they had come to an angry deadlock about in-laws and neither would budge.

When I learned that this dispute had been a weekly occurrence since their honeymoon, I inquired about the rest of their life together. It turned out that they also disagreed regularly about their cocker spaniel, Alex, but in a milder way. Denny allowed the dog to sleep on their bed at night; when Joan objected, he protested that pushing Alex out would cause the dog to feel rejected. I could see that Denny had learned to be much looser than Joan with his emotional boundaries. He was used to those around him doing what they wanted at the expense of his personal space. On the other hand Joan had learned to protect her space, and felt offended by Denny's casualness. When Joan disagreed with his attitude toward his parents, his stubbornness emerged. Neither one would see the other's point.

I suggested an exercise they could do in my office, which could give each a chance to experience the other's point of view. Denny practiced obedience training on Lorelei, as if she were his own dog; this gave him a sense of what it was like to set limits and to say no. I told Joan to take the opposite point of view. I encouraged her to get close to Lorelei by sitting on the floor and seeing how long she enjoyed having Lorelei in her space. During the week they practiced at home with their own dog. By using an animal to help them, Denny and Joan learned how to understand better the other's emotional needs. Talking about and understanding the issues of boundaries and closeness led to a more objective discussion of their differences regarding Denny's parents. Experimenting with their dog taught them that they could play with different positions and still maintain their personal integrity. One did not have to give in to please the other, nor did either need to maintain a rigid, defensive position.

Denny and Joan's case demonstrates the need for recognizing individual differences in marriage. Flexibility comes when each can respect the other's unique point of view. Working with a milder point of contention, the issue of their dog, gave them a nonthreatening way to practice flexibility.

Understanding the Value of Your Differences

Unlike Denny and Joan, who constantly argued about the same few issues, Keith and Betsy, thirty and twenty-nine, respectively, came to therapy because they constantly bickered over every issue. They were too busy complaining to appreciate their individual differences. At their first sessions money was the topic of bickering. Keith felt that money was a safeguard for future security, and Betsy believed that its purpose was to make their present life together enjoyable. They had agreed to buy and furnish their first home, but when they had acquired Geraldine, a lively Afghan hound, the decision of whether to install an expensive fence had been the last straw. Suddenly they had found themselves without compromise. Unfortunately, each had formed a habit of giving in and then harboring resentment. Both of them had felt that they had jeopardized their personal values. They had decided it was time for help.

Keith said they needed an objective opinion about spending $3000 on a fence for their dog. "Betsy has never had a realistic sense of money. Her parents taught her that money was to be spent. She doesn't seem to realize how hard it is to make. Luckily, my dentistry practice has been successful, but we *never* have agreed on the way to spend money."

Betsy interrupted him with unconcealed impatience. "You talk as though I sit home all day and plot ways to spend your money. I work too. Your approach to money has always been stingy. You would think we were on the brink of financial disaster. I have to fight for any major expenditure." She turned to me and continued, "Thank God we've found an animal lover as our therapist. Certainly you'll agree that we need a strong fence for Geraldine."

They both looked at me. I was not foolish enough to give them advice about the fence; I was interested in how they arrived at mutual decisions, and if they respected their differences. The fence just happened to be the issue of the moment. It turned out that they had had many other differences, and one mate had always forced a decision on the less determined one. She chose their furniture and arranged the social commitments. He handled the vacations and watched over the checkbook. They disagreed on sex, so their love life was a disaster. But lately, all their arguments focused on the issue of spending money.

I talked to them about the value of individual differences in marriage. We looked at the characteristics each displayed during their arguments, and found they were the same qualities that had originally drawn them together. For instance, Keith described how he had enjoyed Betsy's lighthearted, playful approach to life when they had first met. He had concentrated so much energy on getting through dental school and building a practice that Betsy had been a treasure. She had brought fun into his overly responsible life. On his thirtieth birthday, for example, she had given him a large, lazy cat, whom he had named Cookie. Both Betsy and Cookie had taught Keith the pleasures of relaxing.

Betsy then told me how she had been attracted to Keith's steadfastness and his conservative values. She had felt that she could depend on him. She had also felt he would be a good father. But she hadn't been able to predict that after living together they would struggle to change each other. She knew that each had forgotten how to appreciate the other. They had to stop trying to change each other. What they both needed was time to listen.

Learning to relax and to listen was helped by the presence of Delilah. She would lay under Keith's feet and look up at him with interest. His voice would soften as he stroked her head. Talking about their courtship helped Betsy and Keith recall how they had once enjoyed those qualities that they now resented. This recognition came as a surprise and allowed them a fresh perspective and renewed sense of humor about the relationship. Focusing on appreciation of their differences rather than criticism of them brought back the excitement they had once shared.

Making a collective decision — whether it is about the price of a new fence or any other issue — is easier when both partners' viewpoints are understood and appreciated.

Exercise Twelve:
Appreciating Your Mate's Uniqueness

This is an exercise to help you remember and appreciate how your lover is different from you.

1. Sit down with your pet and list your spouse's qualities and attitudes that are different from yours. Say some of these qualities out loud to your pet and take notice of how you feel. Give your partner a chance to sit with your pet and to make a similar list of how you are different from him or her.

2. Share your lists with each other. Talk about how these differences add to the richness of your relationship.

3. After you both have had a chance to express appreciation of the other's difference, you can reminisce (as Betsy and Keith did) about how you first fell in love and what attracted you to each other. Picture your spouse on the first day you met. Relive some of that excitement.

4. Take turns sharing these memories. Recall some of the dreams you shared. Soon you'll bring back that magic as you learn to appreciate each other all over again.

Couples do not have to give up their personal values and differences in order to have a successful relationship. Respecting individual values and avoiding the struggle to make your mate be like you encourages richness in a relationship.

Pets are perfect examples of ones who live by this philosophy. They do not expect their masters and mistresses to act like each other or like them. Instead, animals accept different behavior from different family members: a mother might be kind and nurturing, a child might be playful, and so on. The variety of behaviors in the family contributes to the animal's pleasures.

THE BABY DECISION

One conflict many couples face concerns children: should they have them and when. This decision can be complicated by the couple's career involvements and an awareness of the changes that a child would bring to their lives. As a woman faces her biological time clock, she may feel pressured into starting a family. But this may be the time when one career (either hers or his) is at a turning point. In addition, the decisions to give up privacy, independence, and a certain style of living can create a major rift. For some couples these disagreements cloak apprehensions about becoming parents. And some may feel a new role as parent would bring back unfinished emotional issues from childhood. Understanding your mate's point of view about this all-important issue is a stepping-stone to resolving this conflict.

Raising a puppy or kitten is akin to raising a baby. Certainly, some of the problems and decisions are similar. A couple faced with the question of whether to have a child might consider "pet parenting." This is a test to see how well a couple deals with the stresses and responsibilities involved with rearing a little one (of any species). For instance, when a couple adopts a pet, who will get up to let it out? Who will feed it, clean up the mess, decide on its name, and take it to the vet? Who will decide on how much affection and what kind of discipline to give? Making these choices creates a responsibility that will strengthen the level of commitment in any relationship.

Learn To Respect Your Spouse's Needs

When Bruce, thirty, and Patti, twenty-nine, first married, Patti worked as a research technician to support Bruce's medical training. When he finished his residency, she was eager to have a child. Bruce preferred to wait a few years; he wanted them to enjoy their freedom and to get through their financial pressures before they settled into what he termed a domestic rut. Their nightly arguments about this created an icy politeness in their relationship. They entered therapy when they became worried about their marriage.

My dog Delilah welcomed them into the office. I watched Patti cuddle Delilah in a maternal way. When they had settled in, she turned to her husband. "I am tired of running my life to suit your time schedule. For the past four years, you've been a medical zombie. You've kept telling me to wait. Well I've waited. When is it going to be time for me? Even if I got lucky and became pregnant right away, I'd already be thirty by the time the baby came. I want to be young enough to enjoy being a mother."

Patti's voice trembled as she expressed her frustration. She looked hopefully at Bruce, but he was determined to maintain his position. "I'm not going to be pressured into having a baby before I feel ready," he began. "I'm just as weary as you are of my having to study on weekends and constantly be on call. But I've spent most of my life preparing for medicine, and I've finally achieved my goal. Now I'd like a little breather and some time to play. Once the practice gets going, we can start a family."

Patti was not swayed by this logic. "All you think of is yourself, Bruce. What about my needs? This isn't the way you talked *before* we got married." She started to cry. Delilah moved over and put a paw against Patti's leg. Tearfully, Patti rubbed the dog's head, seeking some comfort. She shot Bruce an angry look; neither of them spoke.

It was clear to me that Patti felt betrayed and Bruce felt misunderstood. Luckily, they were both committed to working on the problem and resolving the growing bitterness between them. I suggested they allow themselves a few months of therapy before making any decision. We would work on their listening skills, and they could consider getting a puppy. I described how raising a puppy could provide insight into the responsibilities involved in raising a child. It is a sort of rehearsal. Bruce breathed a sigh of relief, believing he had found a reprieve to their immediate question of whether to have a baby. Patti was less amenable. She said they could look into adopting a puppy, but she didn't want to spend her thirties bringing up a dog.

That weekend they bought a female Newfoundland and named her Priscilla. Bruce, who took to the pet parenting idea better than Patti, was ecstatic. The puppy felt this love from Bruce and returned it in kind. Bruce realized he was a doting "father." If Priscilla was cold or lonely during the night, she was allowed to sleep on his side of the bed. If she needed to go out, it was Bruce who climbed out of bed to accompany her.

Meanwhile, Patti and Bruce continued to work in therapy on learning to communicate. They began to see that part of their impasse with the baby decision had been caused by each wanting his or her own way in the matter. Soon they realized that it was not a matter of someone being right or wrong or someone winning or losing, but a matter of respecting each other's needs. After a few more months, Bruce could better clarify his needs, and he felt less pressured by Patti to change. In addition, in taking care of Priscilla, he had developed a sense of his paternal qualities. He had surprised himself with his patience in taking care of her. During one session he told me that Priscilla helped them feel like a family. They began to talk about having their baby.

Like so many struggling with the decision to have children, Bruce needed time to sort out his feelings. He also needed to experience some typical parenting responsibilities. He had been too busy fighting with Patti to realize that his own fears about being a father contributed to the conflict between them. Patti learned to listen to his feelings of inadequacy; he then felt more accepted and better understood. Their willingness to be open with each other brought them closer together. And their adoption of Priscilla gave them a tangible way to foresee parenthood.

The Fear of Making Mistakes

One couple who came for therapy had no problem deciding that they wanted children, but their trouble came in getting pregnant. Their struggles about this were based on hidden fears. Jeff, thirty-five, and Maggie, thirty-three, had been married four years, and for the past three, Maggie had been trying to get pregnant. They had tried every known method for conceiving. Nothing had worked. Finally, their physician had suggested they consider adoption; but he had recommended they first go into counseling to find out if there were any psychological factors contributing to the problem. Neither of them was enthusiastic about talking to a therapist, but they were willing to try it as a last resort. In fact, they canceled two appointments before they were able to find a time that would work for them. Maggie worked for a television production company and Jeff was a busy attorney. When they walked into the office, Maggie handed me the report from her obstetrician. Then she sat on the couch, some distance away from Jeff.

"We started adoption proceedings last month, and we've been fighting ever since. I can't understand why we suddenly feel the pressure. Jeff, if you had started the fertility tests earlier, it might have been different."

Jeff lit a cigarette and looked at her angrily. "That's ridiculous. You're the one who never has time to make love. You're either involved in meetings or too tired. I don't see how you would find time for a child anyway. You certainly never have time for me."

Jeff and Maggie were assigning blame because fighting each other was easier than looking at their disappointment. When they saw that I was not interested in finding a guilty party, they felt a bit safer. They began to express their fears about becoming parents, and after several months they were able to see how some of their childhood experiences were affecting their attitudes toward parenthood.

I learned that Jeff was the oldest of two children. When his sister had been born, he had suddenly felt emotionally abandoned. He had tried to obtain his parents' attention. Becoming an outstanding student hadn't worked; his parents had seemed more interested in his sister's ballet lessons. (He had been too young to realize that his mother had focused attention on his sister's dancing because of her own thwarted dream of dancing.) He had even chosen the law profession because he had thought it would please his parents. It was only when he had met Maggie that he had regained the feeling of being special. Becoming a father presented a conflict to Jeff. On the one hand he wanted children, but on the other, he unconsciously feared he would lose Maggie's love and attention.

Meanwhile, Maggie was doing her own parental foot dragging. Her parents had been delighted with her performance all through her school years and were proud of her successful career. She knew that Jeff had been attracted to her independence and her ability to stay on top of problems. If they had a child, what would happen if she turned to him for help? Then, too, there had been so much tension between them during the past year that she worried about the marriage breaking up, and being left alone with a young child.

Because both had wasted so much energy harboring hidden fears, the first priority for them was to learn to be honest about their feelings. I recommended that they adopt a puppy. Bowser gave them a chance to test their skills in being clear about their needs. For example, if Maggie got too involved with the puppy, Jeff learned to tell Maggie that he needed her attention. If Maggie was too tired to do her portion of the caregiving, she learned to say so and to ask Jeff to take on the duty. By practicing their listening skills (see Exercise Eleven: Listening to Your Lover, earlier in this chapter) and by using Bowser in a trial run, they developed confidence in their abilities to express their differences regarding time and task. This confidence enabled them to relax. By the end of the year, Maggie was pregnant.

All conflicts concerned with the decision to have a child are not solved simply by having a pet on whom to practice. But adjusting to a new animal in the house is a task that gives a couple the opportunity to talk honestly and to face the needs and differences that emerge in parenting.

Exercise Thirteen: Parent Readiness Quiz

As we have seen, one way to evaluate your willingness and ability to care for a child is to practice rearing a pet. Although some potential parents are not pet lovers, pets and children often require the same type of attention, so if owning a pet is a possibility, this test should help you judge your readiness for children. In other words, this is a fairly reliable way to measure your readiness for parenthood.

Circle the number that best fits your feeling about each question:

AGREE   DISAGREE
5   4   3   2   1

1. *If our pet cries during the night or wakes me up at three in the morning, I tend to its needs.*   5   4   3   2   1

2. *I assume all responsibility for training our pet.*   5   4   3   2   1

3. *If our pet forgets its house training, I clean up the mess.*   5   4   3   2   1

4. *If our pet requests dinner, I immediately feed it and encourage it to enjoy its food.*   5   4   3   2   1

5. *If our pet requires medical attention, I take it to the veterinarian.*   5   4   3   2   1

6. *During flea season I administer the necessary flea baths.*   5   4   3   2   1

7. *I take care of our pet's exercise needs.*   5   4   3   2   1

8. *If our pet knocks over a neighbor's garbage can or causes some other kind of trouble, I approach the neighbor and offer my assistance.*   5   4   3   2   1

Now total your score. What does your score mean?

40–32 points: *You have the potential to be a devoted and committed parent. You understand the responsibilities involved and seem ready to undertake them.*

31–24 points: *You are realistically aware of the responsibilities of parenthood and are willing to be active in that process. You may need a little more time (and perhaps practice with a pet) in order to come to terms with parenthood.*

23 points or less: *You need to reevaluate your interest in starting a family at this time. Practice Exercise Eleven: Listening to Your Lover, so* *you can express your feelings and needs to your partner in an open and comfortable way. Adopting a pet at this time may offer the practice you need for parenthood.*

HOW TO ASK FOR ATTENTION

The success of a relationship depends on how well each person satisfies his or her needs within the marriage while allowing space for the partner to grow. Psychologists Jordan and Margaret Paul, in their book *Do I Have To Give Up Me To Be Loved By You?* (Minneapolis: Comp Care Publications, 1983), talk of the protective circle each partner can build in order to hide a fear of rejection. They describe how partners mistakenly try to avoid the pain of rejection by giving in, trying to control, or becoming indifferent. Working with couples in conflict, I have found that behind the defensiveness there usually is a genuine desire for mutual love and understanding. As a therapist my challenge is to find a way to help two people avoid the destructive pattern of blame and to help them find ways to feel safe enough to reveal their needs for love and attention. I have found in my practice that an accepting pet helps bring this sense of emotional security to lovers as they struggle to resolve their conflicts.

When One Partner Changes

Often one partner changes and begins to move in a different direction from the other. A wife or husband may go back to school, take up a new hobby, learn new skills, meet new friends, or change careers. If children enter a family, one parent may feel left out. During any of these changes, a spouse may begin to feel abandoned. When this happens, admitting the need for attention may be difficult. But for a marriage to be happy and lasting, couples must learn how to make this need be known. If they reach out to one another, their feelings of vulnerability will nurture each other's spirit. Both will grow as they remember that their ability to express love is what brought them together. A perfect model of how to express the need for care and attention is one's pet.

John and Lesley, forty-eight and forty-four, respectively, are a couple in the process of change. When their two daughters had started high school, Lesley had decided to go back to college. At first John had supported her decision, not realizing how much of her energy would go into school. By the end of the first term, John had grown irritable and increasingly critical of her priorities. He had felt pushed aside, but Lesley had developed confidence and excitement in school. Coming home at night and hearing John's complaints had made her question the value of their marriage. Their disagreements had led them to therapy.

John described the problem. "Our house has changed from a comfortable home into Lesley's library. All my wife does is study and worry about exams. I had no idea when she went back for her teaching degree that it would consume our lives. When our daughters come home from school, they are met with a list of chores. Either Lesley is holed up in her room studying, or she's not at home. Many nights Lesley comes home after nine. The girls are suffering. This is not what they need now that they have reached adolescence."

I noted that John had said nothing about his own lack of attention from his spouse. I invited Lesley to express her feelings. While I waited, Delilah sat down beside John and offered him her undivided attention.

Lesley spoke angrily. "You're blowing everything out of proportion! Neither Susie nor Lyn are suffering from anything more than normal teenage moodiness. You were in favor of my getting a teaching degree, and now all I hear are complaints about what a lousy mother I am. It's gotten so bad that I dread coming home, because I know we'll only have another argument. Some nights I go to the library to study, just so I can have some peace and quiet. Besides, why should I be the only one to care for the family? They're *your* daughters too. In another two years I'll be earning a tidy salary and contributing to their college funds. So you can hardly say I've forgotten the girls!"

The debate over the girls' needs could have continued indefinitely, but I knew this wasn't the key issue. At this point John felt abandoned and Lesley was defensive. First we had to address the problems with their relationship. John sat in silence with Delilah by his side. If he stopped petting her for even a moment, Delilah would change position and inch closer so he would continue to stroke her.

I seized the moment. I mentioned to John that Delilah was persistent when she needed attention. I wondered if he didn't feel as Delilah did: in urgent need of attention and love. He admitted that he had felt pushed aside since Lesley had started school. He also admitted that he found it easier to talk about his daughters' needs than his own loneliness. He had had his wife's attention for so many years that he had forgotten how to ask for it. As he began to let Lesley see how rejected he felt, their conversation turned to their needs for intimacy. Lesley then admitted that she had been feeling unjustly accused by John, so that lately she had not wanted to be loving toward him. He described how frightened he felt as she grew away from him; he thought that perhaps soon she would no longer need him.

I suggested that the two of them sit together on the couch and, without talking, John should let Lesley know that he needed her love. He looked a little hesitant until I reminded him of how Delilah had asked for his attention. He smiled, moved closer to Lesley, and put his arm around his wife. They sat for a few moments and communicated nonverbally. On their next visit we worked out a system of organizing the household tasks, so they could spend more time appreciating and enjoying each other's company and that of their daughters.

It is easy for animals to ask for attention. An animal knows *how* to ask for what it wants the *moment* it wants it. For humans it is more difficult. Couples who have been married for awhile sometimes lose the skill of communicating what they need from each other. An especially crucial time to express this need for love is during periods of stress.

Living With Your Mate's Success

Couples experience marital tension if they compete against each other. Ed, fifty-two, and Sandy, forty-six, came to me with just such a problem. When they had first met, Ed had often remarked on Sandy's talent for fabric and clothes design. When she had an opportunity to open a boutique with a friend many years after they had married, Ed had encouraged her. Their sons would soon be in college and Sandy had been ready for a new challenge. Soon after the store's opening, she had received recognition for her innovative designs and the dress orders had piled up. Sandy had been excited and at first Ed had been proud of her. But after a few months, he had begun to stay late at the office. Soon after, he had begun taking his secretary out for dinner. Ed felt left out of his wife's new and successful venture. During therapy they were forced to talk about their feelings and to listen to each other. Sandy admitted she was furious about the attention Ed had been giving his secretary, and her jealousy had made her withdraw from him. As they continued their dialogue, she realized how desperate Ed had been feeling since her store opened and how much he needed her. It was hard for him to ask for attention — he was afraid to let his vulnerability show — but he felt unloved. Fortunately, they were both committed to working on their marriage and rebuilding their bond.

After many sessions they began to listen to each other without making judgments. Now they were ready for the next step: learning how to say, "I need attention." I told them to set aside time to practice at home giving each other nonverbal messages. They got help with this exercise from their cat, Romeo, who never had a problem letting them know when he needed attention. His method: he would lean against someone's leg or jump into an open lap when he wanted to be stroked. When he got what he wanted, he showed his satisfaction with loud purrs. Ed and Sandy watched him and had fun imitating his style. They found it silly but they also realized it was surprisingly easy to get just what they needed from each other without having to say a single word! When they felt mutually loved, their relationship was revitalized, and they found ways to arrange their schedules to be together more often.

Exercise Fourteen: Asking for Attention

This is an exercise to practice your skill at letting your lover know when you want attention. A pet is essential to this exercise.

1. First, spend several days observing your cat or dog, noting its method of getting your attention. See how it watches you and especially how it makes contact when it wants something. (A pet may rub against a leg, put its head in a lap, or give loving looks.) Your pet will let you know instantly when it is pleased.

2. Now find a quiet time to be with your mate. Give a nonverbal message that you want some attention. (Remember your pet's actions from step 1.) Do this slowly. Watch your partner to see how he or she responds to you.

3. Give your partner a chance to communicate a nonverbal message of desiring attention. Alternate turns and see who gets the message first.

4. Let your partner know how much he or she is appreciated, again, nonverbally. Then let your partner take a turn at the same.

5. Next, verbalize your previous nonverbal actions. Have your messages to each other been interpreted properly?

6. Finally, share with each other some of the feelings you have experienced during this exercise. Be sure to express your appreciation of the attention you have given each other. Make a date for another session in the near future. Watch your pet again in the meantime to see if you can pick up any new ideas for nonverbal communication.

This exercise can be a nurturing experience, and watching your pet for tips can be fun. Pets have a natural talent for asking for love. For couples who have a difficult time communicating, this exercise can enrich their relationship.

THE CHALLENGE OF CHANGE AND THE NEED FOR TRUST

The most satisfying relationships are those that create a mutually fulfilling partnership that encourages individual growth and personal change. Breaking established patterns can bring excitement and challenge; it can also bring feelings of anxiety and uneasiness. Unresolved feelings of personal worth may force a couple to reassess their relationship. For some marriages new directions suggest the possibility of separation or divorce. But for those with courage, it can be just the opposite. If couples are flexible enough to allow each other personal growth, a renewed love and trust can evolve. The experience is not always an easy one, but with persistence, it can lead to a stronger relationship.

A perfect model of loyalty and trust is the family pet. Animals offer unquestioning love as they adapt to their family's multitude of changes: new back-to-school hours, out-of-town trips, new professions, or expanding social lives. They never lose faith!

Protecting the Status Quo

Sometimes couples deny each other the opportunity for growth because they are afraid of how these changes may affect their overall relationship. When people feel threatened they often cling to the anchor of steady, predictable habits. In a marriage these patterns can be outmoded and restrictive and in need of loosening up. If one partner pursues a new activity, it does not necessarily mean that he or she plans to leave the marriage. But it can bring worry and protests from the other partner.

This was the problem suffered by Marianne, forty-two, and Gary, forty-four, who, for five years, had been working success-fully on their marriage, the second for each. An excellent sales-woman, Marianne had recently been chosen salesperson of the year by her real estate association. Gary was vice president in charge of finance for a large engineering firm. When Gary had been invited to join a friend in a new consulting firm, Marianne had opposed the move. She had argued that they could not take the risk finan-cially and that he would have to spend too much time on business; she had tried to persuade him to stay where he was. When they entered therapy, the issue was still unresolved.

"Gary doesn't have the personality for his own business. He does wonderfully in the corporate structure, but I know he doesn't excel at independent decisions. For instance, he always leaves our joint decisions up to me. I chose our beach house, and I've ar-ranged every vacation we've ever taken. This is the craziest move he could possibly make. And besides, if this move should fail, Gary's child support payments would drain our savings."

She paused dramatically at this last point, hoping she had persuaded Gary of the folly of his plan. It was obvious that Marianne was feeling threatened by Gary's possible move, but it wasn't yet clear *why* she was afraid. I watched as Gary petted Lorelei, waiting patiently for his wife to finish describing her fears.

Then Gary turned to me and described the financial and other risks involved in this new venture. He knew there would be a period of belt-tightening, but he felt that in the long run the move would benefit both of them. But his detailed analysis and his quiet logic were not what his wife wanted to hear.

As the session continued I sensed that what Marianne feared most was a change in the dynamics of their relationship. True, she was concerned about a change in their standard of living, but more than that, she feared Gary would no longer depend on her emotionally. Although she complained about Gary's lack of decisiveness, she had grown used to making the decisions and taking charge. She knew Gary relied on her judgment and now that reliance was in danger of evaporating. This was one way Marianne had felt emotionally secure in their marriage. Now Marianne needed to feel loved.

As we explored their feelings, it was agreed that psychological work was necessary. Gary needed to stop depending exclusively on his pattern of quiet reason. I suggested pet therapy as a way for him to relax and let out his natural excitement. I suggested he engage their golden retriever, Seabiscuit, in some furious play sessions. In their first venture the two went to the beach, played Frisbee, and rolled on the sand. Seabiscuit encouraged Gary to be both forceful and silly. Dog play turned out to be good therapy for Gary.

Marianne needed to understand Gary's passion for the new venture. But first she had to explore her feelings of emotional insecurity. Her struggles to remain at the top of her field in business combined with her first failed marriage had created an aggressive exterior that protected her deeper feelings of vulnerability. She didn't recognize the fact that Gary cared for more than just her dependability and decisiveness. She struggled to live up to her own high standards, unaware that Gary loved her as she was. He was mature enough to know that all humans have flaws. There was no need for Marianne to protect the status quo of their relationship so vehemently. She finally felt strong enough to reveal her "weaknesses" to Gary. As a result he shared his own deep feelings with her. Gary started the new business with enthusiasm — his own and Marianne's.

Jealousy Versus Trust

It's not unusual for one partner to develop jealousies as a result of the other's change or growth. When this happens the two people must learn to communicate their hidden fears and desires. Norm and Janice, twenty-nine and twenty-seven, respectively, came to see me after their marriage had developed problems. They had been married for two years, were avid tennis players, and were waiting before starting a family. Their only dependent was a cat, Oliver. When Norm's law firm had started sending him out of town on cases, Janice had become critical and moody. Her career as a buyer for women's clothes was in a slump, and she resented him spending so much time away from home. On the verge of starting an affair with her sales manager, she had wisely realized that her marriage came first.

During their first session Janice did most of the talking. She admitted to Norm that she was jealous of his time away and had even considered having an affair. She described how miserable she had felt as she had imagined him on a business trip becoming sexually involved with an attractive female associate. Janice was embarrassed about her fantasies, but she was desperate enough to admit them to her husband. Norm listened without criticism. Being away from home had not been easy for him either. He had neglected to tell her of his fantasies about *her* possible infidelities. Neither one had felt safe enough to talk of internal fears or feelings of insecurity. They had each assumed that if the topic of infidelity was brought up, it might lead to its occurrence. In the weeks that followed, they practiced listening exercises, first with their cat and then with each other. Both confronted their fears and feelings of vulnerability. They realized that after sharing their thoughts, a stronger bond of trust was developed.

BUILDING TRUST AND COMMITMENT

If couples are open with each other, they will find opportunities to build a bond of mutual commitment. Changes can add to the richness in any marriage; the partners must trust one another. An animal is a perfect example of this type of instinctive faith and trust. By observing your pet's unconditional love for you, you can learn to build this same sense of trust in your partner.

Guidelines for Building Trust

Here are some suggestions to help you encourage growth within your marriage and to increase your mutual trust during periods of change.

1. Be aware that it is natural for partners to change at different times and at different rates.

2. Do not assume that your mate's new excitement or interest indicates an inadequacy on your part. You cannot be all things to your spouse.

3. If you notice that you are uneasy about new developments, practice Part One of Exercise Eleven: Listening to Your Lover. After you have clarified your need move on to Part Two by sharing these thoughts with your mate.

4. Allow time for both of you to express your feelings about any change. Reaffirm your commitment to each other.

5. Use the experiences and feelings from this conflict to build a stronger bond of trust and commitment for the future.

6. Realize that you also have the opportunity to seek growth. The more each of you brings to the relationship, the richer your marriage will become.

SUMMARY

Couples begin a relationship appreciating what they have in common. Conflicts arise when they begin to disagree about these common values. Most times these conflicts concern domestic roles, time schedules, in-laws, sex, professional demands, or children. Outside obligations can cause one spouse to feel threatened and unloved. Minor irritations in a marriage do not need to escalate into major confrontations. As partners make individual changes, attention and care from a mate becomes a priority. Empathetic listening helps lovers to share and stay open to each other during periods of stress. Pet therapy can be a way for two partners to solve conflict. Pets can lighten tension and can create opportunities to relax so partners can have a rational perspective on the issues. Pets can serve as models to lovers on how to ask for what is needed. Pets also can be used effectively in making a decision whether to bear children. In sum, a strong sense of trust and commitment is the most important factor in keeping a marriage happy and stable. The two partners must work together to effect this harmony, and pet therapy at key instances can assist in the process.

CHAPTER FIVE

Parenting A Happy Child

A child and a pet is a natural pairing. Research shows that more than half of all American families have one or more pets. Animals serve as a source of pleasure, provide a catalyst for exercise, and offer security and protection. Pets teach children a respect for life, and allow them to experience the giving and receiving of love. According to British veterinarian Bruce Fogel, the pet acts as a window to its family (*Pets and Their People* [New York: Penquin Books, 1983]). In other words, it provides an essential link in family relationships. This is especially important because the traditional nuclear family has undergone a major transformation since the late 1960s. No longer does a typical family unit contain two parents and two children. Instead, millions of American households are headed by single parents.

Animals can provide assistance to children in their growth and development. If given the chance, children gain a sense of control and confidence when accompanied by a pet. Animals offer support to children as they move into each stage of change. For example, an animal can encourage a toddler to explore the environment and release energy in play. A pet can help a school-age child build a social bridge to other children, thus increasing the child's learning and verbal skills. The animal's nonjudgmental acceptance enhances self-esteem. Studies show that children and adolescents confide in their animals, and believe their pets are sensitive to their feelings. The long-standing affectionate bond between child and animal naturally will allow the pet to take on an unofficial role as therapist, as we will see. In addition, taking care of the pet teaches responsibility and fosters self-discipline. When a child has a pet, a friend and companion is always available. Training a dog in obedience can help heighten a child's self-discipline, concentration, and sense of ease in the world. Children who are lonely or shy receive empathetic love from their animals. Pets also encourage creativity. The task of parenting a happy child is made easier with the help of the family pet.

Research Studies Support the Importance of the Child – Pet Bond

In 1968 Boris Levinson, an early pioneer in research on children and animals, reported on successful results with animal-facilitated therapy conducted with emotionally disturbed children. (These findings are reported in two books: *Pet-Oriented Psychotherapy* [Springfield, Ill.: Charles C. Thomas, 1969] and *Pets and Human Development* [Springfield, Ill.: Charles C. Thomas, 1972].) Levinson found that children looked on the animals as accepting of, and dependent on, them; therefore the children felt safe and were able to express feelings that they heretofore had not been able to share with adult therapists. He found that not only could an animal perform a role as therapist to a child, but a pet's constancy contributed to a decrease in a child's emotional problems.

Child psychologist Lee Salk, in *The Complete Dr. Salk: A to Z Guide to Raising Your Child* (New York: New American Library, 1983), states that children are treated like special people by their pets. Pets don't scold, don't nag, and don't expect a clean room. They just give love and respect.

In 1984 *Psychology Today* conducted a survey on the relationship between pets and people; there were 13,000 responses. Almost 100 percent of the respondents indicated that pets were important in the development and socialization of children, and that a child should have a pet. The respondents offered three main reasons for this opinion: (1) pets provided companionship and pleasure; (2) pets taught gentleness; and (3) pets taught responsibility. It was also felt, by seven out of ten, that owning a pet was helpful in understanding the responsibilities involved in parenting (Jack C. Horn and Jeff Meer, "The Pleasure of Their Company: A

Report on *Psychology Today*'s Survey on Pets and People," *Psychology Today* [August 1984]).

In my experience as a psychologist, I have worked with countless families in therapy. In addition, I have directed parent workshops on children's relationships to the family pets. In my research and interviews, I have found that animals and children have a special bond that contributes to healthy learning. From the moment the child meets the animal, the pet can serve as a teacher, friend, *and* therapist.

PUTTING CHILD AND PET TOGETHER

The first contact between a baby and an established family pet will be the start of a nurturing relationship. But careful planning is a must, because sibling rivalry is not limited to children. If you have a dog or a cat that has enjoyed top billing in your home, there is a potential for jealousy. To avoid such problems, use the pointers below as a guideline to the smooth introduction of pet and child.

Guidelines for Introducing Pets and Newborns

1. Before the baby arrives expose the dog or cat to children of all ages, but especially to small infants.

2. Accustom the pet to the sound of a baby's cry. If you can't arrange for a real baby to visit, bring home an audio tape to play for the animal.

3. Expose the dog or cat to all types of baby items that will be brought into the home, that is, noisemakers, toys, clothes, and so on.

4. Introduce your pet to the smells that it will associate with the baby. Bring the pet into the nursery, and let it smell the powder and new baby furniture. Before the baby arrives you might want to bring home a dirty diaper, so the pet may be introduced to the newborn's scent.

5. Correct obedience problems now, for example, a dog jumping up on people or forgetting its "stay" command.

6. Stock up on extra pet toys and treats for use during the first few weeks.

7. Be patient with your pet. Some animals, like older siblings, revert to childhood and need to be housebroken again. This will pass with retraining and patience.

8. Put the crib up before the baby arrives, and train your cat to stay out of it. Use a squirt gun with water to discourage its entering. (If you do not want the cat to sleep with the baby, you must train your cat to stay away from the sleeping child.)

9. Be present at all times that pet and child are together. Your presence will ensure stability between the two new friends, and will also give you peace of mind.

Then comes the big day! Of course you may have your own way of dealing with this situation, but here are some ways other parents have handled the special day. One father carried the new baby into the house while the mother spent a few minutes alone with the dog, playing with it and giving it a treat. Another mother introduced her poodle to their son, who lay on the couch. She let the dog smell the baby's feet and hands, but did not let the animal near her son's face. The dog was puzzled for a day or so, but then got used to its new friend. In fact, the baby loved it when the dog kissed his toes, and would respond by laughing and reaching for the poodle. Another couple found that their Labrador retriever needed extra attention after the baby's arrival. For them the situation was akin to having a second child come into the house. The father had to take the dog out for extra playtime and otherwise lavish more attention on the animal, and eventually the tension relaxed. In another case a mother's Abyssinian cat had been the only "child" for several years before the baby was born. Because she was a single mother, it was particularly important to her that the cat and baby get along. The new mother carefully nurtured the baby – pet bond by calmly stroking the cat every time she held her child. The cat became fascinated by the baby, and would even fetch the mother when the infant cried! These relationships got off to healthy starts because of careful planning on the part of the parents.

Adopting the Pet

If your petless family is ready to assume responsibility for an animal's care, there also are points to consider. Adopting a pet into a family is like introducing a new person (baby or stepparent, for instance) into the family. Proper planning and the involvement of all family members can turn a potentially negative situation into a loving, learning experience. There are several steps necessary for the smooth integration of pet into family.

Each member of the family should be a part of the selection process. A family conference is the best way to manage democratic decision making. (When deciding on a family pet, often a hurried choice is made, without thought to gender, breed, or care; a hasty decision, however, could lead to problems for both the pet and its family.) The family conference gives the children added incentive to carry out responsibility, and it also averts anger or blame if the answer is not what they wish.

As an example of how well democratic decision making works, one of the mothers I spoke with told me that her daughter, Tracy, ten, had learned that the family down the street had a pregnant basset hound. Of course she wanted one of its puppies. She knew that her father would not be in favor of the new addition as the family already had a cat, and he often said that one pet was enough, but she asked her mother anyway. Wisely, her mother suggested a family conference, during which Tracy could argue her case. Her mother encouraged Tracy to prepare properly, because her father's opinion was a tough one to change. Tracy went to the library and gathered information on the breed and the costs of its care. She brought all her arguments to the conference and even devised a petition for pet ownership and care, which follows. Tracy's father was impressed by his daughter's mature approach to the situation. He changed his vote and the puppy was adopted.

What kind of pet is best depends on the way of life of the family. Selecting the right pet is part of the learning experience. Of course each family member may have his or her own preference. Allow these differences to be discussed; a good discussion serves as a model for open communication. But be aware of the practical considerations. If there are preschoolers in the house, an easygoing, friendly dog is preferable to a skittish one. Also, with a very young child, a kitten younger than four months might not be a wise choice, as it is likely to take attention away from the child and resentment results. If the family chooses a cat, the children get an opportunity to discover the independent spirit of the feline. In addition, caregiving is not as involved. If the family's choice is a dog, each member will be more involved in the animal's training and care.

When the day arrives to bring the pet home, be sure to use your children in helping the animal adjust to its new environment. Have your child locate a space for the pet (an animal's own area is just as important as a child's need for a room of his or her own). A cat will want a scratching post; it may like to sleep up high. A dog will need a bed of its own.

The first veterinary visit is as important for your child as for the pet. Certainly your child will learn from it. When selecting a vet, be certain to choose one who is patient and who understands the needs of your pet and the curiosity of your child. If the veterinary visits are treated without a lot of emotion, your child will be stimulated by the experience instead of frightened.

If difficulties arise over the pet's care, another family conference is in order. Of course the responsibilities outlined should be taken seriously, but flexibility is needed if a child's grades or social schedule begin to present conflicts. Rearranging and compromising is all part of life.

Petition for Pet Ownership

Below is a sample of a petition for pet ownership and care. You may want to use this as a model when creating a contract for the care of your own pet.

> I, _____ request that a (dog/cat/other animal) _____ become a member of our family. I request that I be part of the selection process, that I be able to suggest its name, and that I be allowed to help take care of this pet. I would be willing to feed the pet on (day) _____, at (time) _____. I promise to exercise our pet daily by taking it outside to play. I request that I take part in the obedience training. I will need help from others in the family for the following duties:
>
> _____
> _____ .
>
> I have talked to these family members, and they have agreed to help in those areas.

This contract is to be reviewed weekly, and at the end of one month, it may be rewritten by me. If this contract is not fulfilled, it will be brought to family conference for discussion and action.

Petitioner's Signature _____

Other Family Members' Approval _____

Date _____

A Caveat Regarding Unfamiliar Pets

Parents should train children to behave properly around strange animals. Until youngsters have experience with, and the proper judgment to approach, unfamiliar animals, here are some guidelines that will be helpful in avoiding difficulties:

1. Your child should never approach a strange animal without parental supervision.

2. Your child should not try to stop two animals from fighting, even if one is the family pet.

3. Teach your child to offer an upturned palm when meeting a new dog; this gesture tells the dog that the child is friendly and not a threat.

4. Children should be told never to approach a strange animal while it is eating or sleeping.

Anticipating and guarding against potential problems can prevent an unnecessary negative experience that could affect a child's relationship with his or her own pets.

HOW A PET CAN HELP
WITH SIBLING RIVALRY

Often a child's first pangs of jealousy are felt when a new baby is introduced into the home. But this hurtful feeling can be minimized with proper anticipation. Certainly, the older child will need special attention, and this may be the time to use a pet. If you already have a family pet, use the animal as a model to discuss the feelings of jealousy *it* may feel because of the newborn's arrival, being sure to describe the same feelings your own child might be experiencing. If you don't have a pet, this might be a good time to get one. If your child is at an age when he or she is longing for some responsibility, introducing a new pet before the baby is born will ameliorate some of the feelings of jealousy your child is likely to experience. You can let your child be responsible for a good portion of the animal's care. This has a twofold advantage: besides teaching your child to give the pet proper care, you also will be teaching your child about the new baby's needs by giving him or her a chance to become familiar with the pet's needs before the new sister or brother comes home.

After the baby's arrival the pet will be there to continue to offer love and special attention to the older child. You may note that after the newborn's arrival, the older child may appear to lose some of his or her independence; if you have a pet, the child may become closer to the animal by having long conversations or taking extra playtime with the dog or cat.

Just such a situation occurred with Ellen, who was seven when her mother explained that a new baby was soon to enter their family. Ellen was excited about the prospect, and her parents gently involved her in the preparations. She never had been close to the family's Shetland sheepdog, but her mother noticed a sudden change in this relationship right after Ellen's brother was born. After the excitement of the baby's arrival had subsided, and Ellen realized she was not the only child in the family anymore, she looked to the dog for much needed attention and love. The dog responded to Ellen's extra love by returning it in kind. In fact, Ellen's mother was surprised and touched to hear Ellen explain to the dog that they shouldn't feel sad about not getting as much attention anymore, because the new baby needed it more than they did. The dog's presence became a comfort to Ellen and offered her security during this time of transition.

On the other hand, if your youngest child feels jealous of your older children, a pet's presence can help temper these painful feelings. Caring for an animal properly is one job that a child can perform well, bringing him or her to an equal level with an older sibling.

Decreasing Sibling Rivalry

To decrease the feelings of sibling rivalry, here are some guidelines parents can follow.

1. If the situation concerns a newborn's arrival, be sure to give the older child extra attention. Introduce a new hobby or other form of amusement that will give the child a feeling of accomplishment. In addition, give the older child extra privileges, such as the privilege to stay up later.

2. If the child (older or younger) expresses negative feelings, encourage him or her to describe these feelings and pay careful attention to what the child is telling you.

3. Don't compare children. Instead, encourage the attitude that each is unique.

4. Separate their possessions, including their pets. If possible, let each have his or her own (dog, cat, fish, lizard, and so on).

5. Separate them when they fight. Don't try to decide who was wrong. Let them know you have confidence that they can solve their disagreements, but make the limits clear about unacceptable behavior. Suggest they talk to a pet about the problem. Once the disagreement is aired, it's often easier to find a solution.

PETS THROUGH A CHILD'S PRESCHOOL YEARS

A pet's presence can help in the preschool years (that exciting time when children begin to explore and learn about their ever expanding world). Encouraging your toddler to play with an accepting, loving animal will widen your child's scope during this period. For example, pets serve as useful models for the toddler in forming positive relationships. In addition, touching and talking to the animal develop in the child the feelings of warmth, security, and love, which are critical in these years. Animals also serve as incentive for movement. Often a baby will follow a cat's movements with the eyes and then will try the same movement. A pet's presence is particularly helpful during the child's crawling stage, and later when the child learns to walk.

One mother described the pleasure her son Rick, two, got from the family's Sealyham terrier, and how the dog was actually a help in Rick's developing his verbal skills. The boy liked to "talk" to the dog during breakfast. Naturally, the dog "talked" back. Rick learned his first word, *woof*, after listening to the dog bark. Rick also used the dog to develop his tactile sense; as an infant, he would lay beside the dog and cuddle with it until both were contentedly asleep. Another mother told me that her infant's first attempt to walk was with the help of their golden retriever. The baby would gently grab onto the dog's coat and pull herself up. Then the two of them would carefully step around the house.

Pets are also an excellent means for teaching children socialization concepts, such as gentleness and respect. Using the pet as a model, you can explain that living things need to be respected. Begin by telling the child not to do anything to the animal that would hurt it. In teaching your child to respect others, make the limits clear. Setting guidelines for your child's treatment of the pet will give your toddler a sense of security. By the time your child is two, he or she may want to test the rules. Simply remind your child of the limits, and encourage him or her to talk gently to the pet. Having your child converse in a gentle way helps him or her to develop empathy and verbal skills. (Most children, like adults, feel that their pets understand what is being said.) This kind of empathy taught at an early age will help the preschooler develop socialization skills.

Two-and-a-half-year-old Sunny needed to learn how to be gentle with the family's Labrador retriever. After learning to walk she became rough with the animal, pulling at its tail and tugging at its ears. But Sunny's mother instigated gentleness training as soon as she noticed Sunny's rough treatment. After a series of quiet reminders from her mother, Sunny stopped being rough with the dog and even boasted that she had learned how to be nice.

Matti's father had been around dogs his whole life, and he wanted his daughter to have the same positive experiences. One of the things he did was to teach his five-year-old how to watch their dog's body, thereby learning from the sounds and movements how the dog was feeling. Thus, Matti was introduced at an early age to the concept of nonverbal communication.

At age two Jill had been around her family's two Doberman pinschers all her life. But she had developed normal childhood fears: she sometimes was frightened of monsters, loud sounds, or new faces. Because of her familiarity with the dobies, she naturally felt safer having one of the dogs near her. Now at age three she refers to her dogs as sisters and enjoys visiting the other pets in the neighborhood with them. Her mother believes that Jill's attachment to the dogs helped her get over her fears, while teaching her respect for living things; she also feels that the dogs improved her daughter's communication skills.

Pets also teach the young child patience. For example, Coleman, who was an active and intense four-year-old, was given a tortoise for his birthday. He would lay out the pet's food, and naturally it would take a long time for the animal to arrive! Coleman would stamp his feet and show other signs of impatience, but slowly he began to understand the tortoise's natural movements. His mother described this as her son's first lesson in patience.

The feelings of love and security that toddlers receive from their mothers are often transferred to toys (a teddy bear is a prime example). But having your child transfer love to a pet is also a good choice, for animals make children feel safe when parents are not there, provide undivided attention, and give unadulterated love. A child often treats a pet in the same way the child is treated. If you listen in on a conversation, you will hear the child imitating the parents as he or she talks to the pet; the child will say, "Bad kitty!" or "Good dog!" Promoting a link between child and pet will help your toddler recognize his or her individuality as he or she works out feelings toward those in the environment. Children eventually learn from these feelings and thoughts and thus earn a sense of self-esteem. This in turn influences later stages of growth.

TEACHING RESPONSIBILITY: A PET'S THE PERFECT WAY

All parents with whom I have dealt have been concerned about teaching their children a sense of responsibility. The first thing some parents do to achieve this goal is to obtain a family pet. Many parents believe that having a pet will automatically offer responsibility to the child; this is mostly true, but parents must be careful not to fall into some common traps.

For example, the child at first may be quite happy to care for the pet, but then a parent may end up caring for the animal completely. How does this transference of responsibility happen? Child psychologist Haim G. Ginott, Ph.D., believes that giving children a *voice* in those matters that affect them is the key to developing a realistic sense of responsibility (*Between Parent and Child* [New York: Macmillan, 1965]).

If you do decide to teach responsibility with the aid of a family pet, you can begin by having your child sit in on the selection process (see "Putting Child and Pet Together" earlier in this chapter). As a parent you will have certain preferences regarding breed, price, size, upkeep, and temperament, but your child should be allowed to voice his or her opinion. Help your child gather information, photos, and reading material, and take him or her to dog or cat shows, so he or she can effectively join in the selection process. This is a healthy way for your child to achieve responsibility for the pet, besides having a good time!

Kurt, age five, had watched the mother cat next door birth kittens, and he desperately wanted one of his own. Before his parents consented they talked to him about helping with the feeding and grooming; he would share equal responsibility for the cat with his mother and father. (His parents rightfully and logically did not demand that he be the sole caregiver.) Of course he was eager to take part. What made the experience particularly effective for Kurt was the "kitty care rehearsal." Kurt learned where the cat dish, cat food, and cat brush would be kept. Once a day he would practice his duties as if the cat were really there. A calendar was set up and his days and duties were clearly marked, so he could cross off each chore as it was completed. Kurt selected the kitten himself (he identified the gentlest one by holding it upside down and seeing how relaxed it was), and he even chose its name. One of Kurt's duties was to choose the cat food. He experimented with different brands, and felt very important performing his chore. Kurt came to enjoy grocery shopping, a previously boring activity for him. His parents offered much praise; when he shirked one of his chores, they quietly reminded him. His parents emphasized the positive aspects of Kurt's kitty care and it turned out to be a pleasurable and valuable experience for all.

Guidelines for Teaching
Responsibility to Your Child

Here are some guidelines to help teach your child responsibility, whether it's with the family pet or with some other type of household chores.

1. Allow your child to choose the task for which he or she would like to be responsible.

2. Define as exactly as possible what this job is, all the while understanding your child's capabilities.

3. Set up the task with your child so that he or she will have an optimal opportunity to succeed.

4. Be sure your child knows when to perform the chore and when it has been completed.

5. Set up an evaluation period for you and your child. Be prepared to make amendments if, say, the duties are too difficult or the time schedule is inconvenient. (The evaluation period is not only helpful with your child's pet-related responsibilities, but it sets up a method of thinking that can be useful in school and later in adult life.)

6. Don't perform your child's duties! If your child gradually loses interest in his or her responsibilities, think up ways to keep the tasks interesting, or reward your child every month or so for a job well done.

7. Praise your child when he or she fulfills responsibilities. This is important to your child's developing a sense of pride in his or her work.

HELPING YOUR CHILD FEEL SECURE

Studies done at the Gesell Institute for Child Behavior show that children have predictable fear patterns at different ages. For instance, the two-year-old may be frightened of noises such as thunder and wind. At two and a half the fear may be over changes in household routines, such as Daddy coming into the house via a different door or Mommy rearranging the living room furniture. At three fears of the dark and of burglars may emerge. At four a fear over parents departing, first seen in very early childhood, may resurface (Frances L. Ilg, Louise B. Ames, and Sidney M. Baker, *Child Behavior: From the Gesell Institute of Human Development* [rev. ed.][New York: Harper and Row, 1981]).

The presence of the family pet can serve as a security blanket when a child is momentarily frightened. According to Alan Beck, Sc.D., and Aaron Katcher, M.D., a family pet offers the child a feeling of safety and keeps him or her engaged without the constant presence of, and reassurance from, the parents. Pets give children warmth, security, and the opportunity to use their imaginations in dreaming up situations, which in turn helps the child define an identity separate from that of the mother or father (*Between Pets and People* [New York: G. P. Putnam's Sons, 1983]).

Four-year-old Julie had trouble getting to sleep at night; she was afraid she might have nightmares. As a possible solution her parents let her choose a part-terrier mutt at Pet Orphans. She and the dog became inseparable. She played house with the dog during the day, and when she went to bed at night, the dog would sit beside her while her parents read her a bedtime story. The dog's presence brought Julie a sense of security that was particularly manifested at night. Because the dog stayed with her until she fell asleep, over a period of time, her nightmare problem disappeared.

Using Your Pet To Help Combat Fears

Following are some ways you can use your family pet to help your daughter or son overcome common childhood fears.

1. Encourage your child to spend lots of time with the pet, thus developing a strong bond of love and friendship. Having a pet therapist available for the little fears could keep these fears from growing out of proportion.

2. Encourage your child to hold and talk to the pet about a fear. If *you* respect the fear, it will subside more quickly. Especially, don't imply that your child's fear is wrong or babyish.

3. Reassure your child that when you are away for a time, the pet is there to look after him or her.

ENHANCING YOUR CHILD'S SELF-ESTEEM

Self-esteem is defined as a person's confidence and how he or she judges himself or herself. Dorothy Briggs, author of *Your Child's Self-Esteem* (New York: Doubleday, 1970), believes that this attitude is the most important factor in slating a child for success or failure as an adult. In order to attain self-esteem, a child must believe that he or she is lovable, unconditionally accepted, and valuable. A child must also believe that he or she is worthwhile, competent, and can master the environment.

Because unconditional love, that is, love without any prior conditions, is crucial to self-esteem, it is important that parents understand that they — and the family pet — both have the opportunity to offer this love to the child. When parents show a baby their happiness and interest, the baby takes this positive image and begins to create a picture of himself or herself. When they show excitement and pleasure in a child's actions, that child's sense of pride is developed. A child builds a sense of self-worth based on what is transmitted by the family. When a child sees himself or herself as capable and lovable, he or she learns to act in just this way. The child begins to believe in the love he or she receives and also believes he or she can succeed in life.

On the other hand, a feeling of low self-esteem also is learned from the messages a child takes in from the family. If a child receives criticism (verbally or nonverbally) when he or she experiments with new things, his or her self-esteem will suffer from these negative messages. When this happens the child can become self-critical and self-demanding, afraid to try new situations. A child needs to receive loving messages, or else he or she will begin to question his or her own lovability, and his or her sense of self-esteem will suffer. There is no better way to offer unconditional love than by putting child and pet together.

Eric, at five years, was considered by his parents as unnaturally withdrawn. Although test results showed he was extremely bright, his parents were worried about his listlessness and his lack of desire to communicate with either peers or parents. But just before Eric started kindergarten, his parents bought him a Welsh corgi. There were no children living on his street, so the two became friends out of necessity. In the beginning Eric was rough with the dog, but with cajoling from his parents, Eric learned to be gentle and kind. The dog rewarded this change in behavior with more attention. Soon enough child and dog were best of friends; the first thing Eric would do when he came home from school was call out for his friend, and the two of them would launch into a furious play session. One thing Eric noticed about the dog was that it never asked him questions or expected any conversation at all! Eric could feel loved without having to say anything. Eventually, Eric began to open up to the dog, and he would have long talks with it. By the time Eric had finished his year in kindergarten, he had relaxed with his classmates. This behavioral change was a direct consequence of his play sessions and chats with the corgi.

Lucy came to me for therapy when she was a teenager. She was withdrawn and lonely. She had no confidence in her ability to make friends, and so rather than risk rejection, she did without. But both of her parents worked, and Lucy found herself at home by herself for a good portion of every day. It was not hard for me to discern that Lucy had a problem with self-esteem. She needed to build her confidence. But how? During one session she offhandedly mentioned her cat. I learned that Lucy found comfort in the cat's presence, but she did not know how to use it. I suggested she begin by giving her cat lots of extra love and attention. Lucy followed my suggestion and the cat responded well. Soon Lucy began to feel secure and, more important, loved. If Lucy was home sick from school, her cat would offer comfort. If she did poorly on a test, she would confide this to her pet. Lucy began to feel special; this feeling was directly linked to the pure love her cat showed her. And as a result she felt more comfortable with herself and then was able to make new friends.

Dog obedience training is an ideal "parenting" activity for youngsters. A child gets a feeling of self-worth from giving affection and education to a pet. A child will feel less anxious about his or her own limits if he or she can act as "parent" in dog training. Chris, eleven, had always been a mediocre student. But one of his first feelings of achievement came when he took his Weimaraner puppy to obedience school. The puppy did not learn quickly, but Chris, who was familiar with this type of problem from his own mediocre performance in school, knew just how to handle the dog. He was patient with the dog, never losing his temper. By the end of obedience training, both Chris and the dog had grown from the experience. He was proud of their second-place finish in the class. Chris was given sole credit for the dog's training, and it was the first time he had achieved something so special. Chris's own performance in school even improved as a result of the experience.

Children need to feel special; they need to know they are loved unconditionally. During the maturation years, they need to feel this love, even if they have difficulty with a school task, don't finish their dinner, or leave their room a mess. To avoid the possibility of developing inadequate self-esteem, children need positive messages about their lovability. If they do not get them, it can affect their relationships with family, playmates, and teachers. Loving and demonstrative pets can contribute to this feeling of worth.

HOW DO YOU STIMULATE CREATIVITY?

Creative children are those who bring something new into their lives. They tend to be independent and spontaneous in their approach to problems and active in play. They are highly receptive; they see more, feel more, and listen with more sensitivity than their peers. Frank Barron, who has done extensive research on creativity, believes that the reactions children receive to early attempts at originality determine whether these creative impulses will flourish (*Creative Person and Creative Process* [New York: Holt, Rinehart & Winston, 1969]). There is no evidence indicating that creative children are either maladjusted or lonely. On the contrary, when combined with high intelligence, creative children are successful in achievement and good at social adjustment. They take pleasure in the feeling of mastery that comes from creating something all by themselves.

A child's capability for originality is seen early in life. It starts between ages three and five, before structured learning in school is introduced. At this age, a child is more willing to be different and not so sensitive to peer influence. During these early years parents should promote the child's imagination and sense of fantasy by introducing dramatic play. Pets are perfect for this period of your child's life!

For example, Marcy was four when her mother noticed the beginnings of her artistic talent. Immediately, her mother utilized the family terrier to encourage Marcy's creative spurts. She gave Marcy large sheets of paper, crayons, and pencils and encouraged her to draw pictures of the dog; when she finished, her mother would ask Marcy to show her work to the animal. To Marcy, the dog loved and appreciated everything she drew.

Another mother told me that her daughter, Judy, was seven when she began to show an interest in reading and writing. Again, the child needed a proper subject for her works, and her mother astutely suggested the family cat. This led to an onslaught of poems devoted to feline charms. ("Furred toes and whispering whiskers talk" was a line from her first poem.) Her parents were delighted with these attempts, and Judy's own sense of self-esteem was raised after she received such a positive response.

Children like to create around those things they love. It is no coincidence that many of their early attempts at creativity focus on their pets. They are more likely to try out new ideas if they know in advance that they will not be judged. Pets are the perfect audience for budding creators. Animals are never too busy to come admire a new work. They like the attention and will reciprocate this extra love with some of their own, thus adding to children's confidence.

Danny came to see me when he was eight. His mother was positive of her son's artistic talent and was worried that the boy was too involved with the wrong kinds of activities: all he did in his spare time was watch television or go to the movies. She tried to encourage him to pick up a more productive hobby, but the boy wasn't interested. We decided to try to funnel Danny's two main interests, TV and movies, into a productive hobby. His parents bought him an 8mm movie camera, at the same time introducing a cat and a dog into the family. Danny's life suddenly changed. He began to show his creativity by following the animals around with his camera. Then he got really inspired and would fashion short movies, using the pets as his stars. It was a perfect solution for the boy. Not only did Danny have an outlet for his creativity, but he quit misusing his time.

Some Tips on Promoting Creativity

As parents, you should encourage creativity in your child; you can effect this if you keep the following points in mind.

1. Make sure your child has plenty of free time, so he or she has the opportunity to think up new ideas and experiment with them. Allowing your child solitude will help in the development of imagination.

2. Provide materials for your child, such as clay, paints, felt pens, and paper. Be sure to offer your child guidance in how to use these materials properly.

3. Encourage your child to engage in fantasy play. Pets can be especially helpful here.

4. Don't judge your child's creativity by adult standards.

Creative children show flexibility, autonomy, playfulness, and curiosity. They also have an interest in fantasy, and they pursue their own interests. Parents — and pets — can stimulate a child's creativity, thus adding to the child's overall sense of well-being and self-esteem.

USING YOUR PET TO EXPLAIN BIRTH AND DEATH

One of the benefits of having a pet is the knowledge children acquire about nature through it. Oftentimes a child has no understanding of birth; having an expectant dog or cat can put the process into perspective. Indeed, watching the body change and being present at the birthing is a healthy way for small children to learn about this part of nature. The same is true with death; losing a loved pet will give your child a lesson in accepting an unhappy situation.

Tammi, five, was an only child. She was very attached to her poodle, and was concerned when her dog became quiet and seemed tired. But when Tammi learned that her dog was not sick and that she was soon to be a mother, the child was all smiles. She accompanied her mother on the dog's veterinary visits and was always full of questions. The doctor let Tammi listen to the heartbeats of the puppies, and explained the birthing process to her. Tammi told her mother that she felt very grown up as she witnessed the birth of her dog's seven puppies. Tammi mothered the puppies and got a look at nursing. She kept the runt of the litter as her new puppy. In all, the whole experience was a healthy one for the girl.

Children deal with the loss of their pets in different ways, depending on their age and their experience with separation. The toddler might not even miss his or her playmate, but the school-age child will ask for an explanation of the pet's disappearance.

One of my patients, Jeremy, seven, had lost his dog suddenly. After a day of sadness, he had appeared to accept the loss. A few weeks later, though, he had developed a recurring bad dream in which he saw the dog in his room, but was unable to touch it; inevitably, he would wake up crying. His family realized that he had not expressed his feelings completely enough to fully resolve the loss. We sat together and talked about his dog's death. After a time he was able to explain his secret fear that his parents might die and leave him too, just like his dog had. When he could talk about the loss and his anxiety over it, his bad dreams disappeared.

Helping Your Child Deal With Loss

Children respond to the death of a pet with the same stages of grief that adults experience, which include denial, sadness, anger, and finally, letting go. They may exhibit symptoms such as nightmares, insomnia, anger toward parents (or veterinarians), or guilt. If these problems are allowed to persist, they may create even deeper problems for your child. Following are activities designed to help your child deal with the loss of a pet.

1. Encourage your child to put his or her feelings into words; this may be hard, but it is important for your child's health to purge the hurtful feelings before they become too deeply-rooted.

2. Encourage your child to draw a picture of the pet or to make a scrapbook using photos of the animal.

3. Talk about the enjoyable experiences your child shared with the pet. This helps your child say good-bye and gives him or her a more realistic way to deal with the loss.

4. Have your child write a poem or story about the pet. This is a constructive, creative outlet for grief that helps with the emotional healing.

When the child is ready (the waiting period is different for each child), a new pet can be brought in to fill the gap left by the departed friend. Sometimes the child will want the same breed, but a different color; another may want to switch to a different animal altogether. In any event don't push the child into making a hasty decision.

It is difficult to explain such concepts as birth or death to a child. But learning about these two facets of nature through the family pet gives a child a foundation of reality and a way of communicating his or her feelings with the family.

HELP YOUR CHILD COPE WITH STRESS OR LONELINESS

In my experience with parents and children, I have found one outstanding feature in the relationships between pets and children: in most cases, the dog or cat was used as a confidante in times of change, stress, or loneliness. A research study was performed by Thomas E. Catanzaro, D.V.M., in which nine hundred military couples indicated how important the family pet was to the physical and emotional health of their children. Results showed that the children felt their pets understood what was spoken to them. They also believed the pets were sensitive to their moods, stayed close to them during periods of anxiety or sadness, and provided support during times of crisis, such as divorce or death (Thomas E. Catanzaro, "The Human–Animal Bond in Military Communities," in *The Pet Connection*, ed. Robert Anderson, Benjamin Hart, and Lynette Hart [Minneapolis: Center to Study Human–Animal Relationships and Environments, University of Minnesota, 1984]).

Children respond to change differently, but most will exhibit some form of anxiety or stress during times of change. Some may become overly dependent on parents as they search for security, and others may become disciplinary problems. In times of change or stress, the family pet can function as a constant, helping relieve the child's uneasiness.

If a family move is approaching, for instance, a pet's presence can be soothing for the child. The preschooler won't understand why he or she must leave familiar surroundings. It is hard for a child to express feelings about the sudden upheaval in his or her life. But the family pet is familiar and will give the anxious child a feeling of security and a chance to physically hold on to someone he or she loves and to whom he or she can talk. (For a period after the move, special attention from both parent and pet is a help in preventing a long-term problem.)

The school-age child faces his or her own particular problems during a time of change. Leaving school and friends behind and meeting strangers can be stressful. Again, a loving pet can offer reassurance during this transition. Besides offering comfort and familiarity, the animal can be a means through which the child can socialize with new children in a spontaneous way.

If Your Child Undergoes a
Stressful Situation

Rita was four when her family moved. Her mother, Louise, sought my help because with the change, her daughter had become withdrawn, clingy, and fearful of her new nursery school; ultimately, she had become afraid to go to sleep at night. I suggested to Louise that she set about to make her child's new environment more enjoyable, and perhaps adopting a pet for Rita might be the answer. She heeded my advice and bought a lop-eared rabbit for her daughter. Then Louise invited the neighborhood children to their home, knowing that the bunny would be the big attraction. And it was! Rita began to look forward to these neighborly get-togethers. She felt proud that hers was the only rabbit on the block. She relaxed and slowly began to enjoy her new surroundings. With the help of her pet therapist, Rita became more confident in her home and neighborhood and began to come out of her shell.

Even more traumatic than a family move is divorce or death. The child must adjust to new living arrangements and, in the case of divorce, often is put in the middle of parental arguments. Sometimes the child feels responsible for the death of a parent or for the breakup of the marriage. Besides external forces, the child must deal with complex internal struggles. A family pet certainly can help temper this kind of trauma. The pet offers unconditional love, reassurance, and attention. When the child needs a confidante, the pet will be there to listen.

When Jonathan was nine his parents divorced. Two years later his mother remarried; his father remarried shortly after that. Jonathan began to spend one weekend a month with his father, whose new wife had two children. Naturally, Jonathan was upset and anxious over these changes in his life. His mother, who knew that he had always been close to his cat, encouraged him to spend more time with it. He would take it to his room and talk with it. Its purring made him feel more relaxed and more loved. At the same time he developed an attachment to the family dog at his father's house, a lovable cocker spaniel. Jonathan's mother told me that both pets made him feel special. It was more than a year before Jonathan adjusted to all the family changes, but the pets in both families helped him through this stressful period.

Helping Your Child To Cope With Change

What can you do to help your child during a period of change? Following are a few suggestions to consider.

1. Keep your child well informed of all upcoming changes.

2. Involve your child in decisions, however small, so he or she can exercise some control over changes.

3. Encourage the expression of feelings. Allow time for questions or discussions.

4. Keep family routines (mealtimes, bedtimes, chores, and so on) as regular and consistent as possible.

5. Allow the family pet to offer security and constancy. Let the pet's adjustment to change serve as a model for the child.

6. Encourage your child to reach out to new friends, utilizing the pet in this endeavor whenever possible.

7. Provide love and stability while your child readjusts.

Avoiding Loneliness

During the past fifteen years, the family unit has changed dramatically. There are more single parents and working mothers than ever before, and as a result, an increasing number of children are left alone during daytime hours. Children today who must fight loneliness often turn to their pets. The children I treat who are trying to deal with loneliness and who own animals tell me they share everything with their pets, including talks, walks, meals, and naps. In fact, some of their parents were surprised to learn that their children had long conversations with their pets. Many of my younger patients reveal to me that they talk to their pets whenever they are upset about school or feel left out of some social event. They believe their pets understand their feelings. They also claim that there are times when their animals are better listeners and offer more comfort than their parents do.

One of my patients, Neil, was a middle child in his family and the only boy. He often felt rejected by his parents and left out by his two sisters. Mostly, he felt lonely. When he was able to express his feelings to his parents, they decided to remedy the situation with a family pet. Neil became quite attached to the male boxer they bought: after all, they were the only two "boys" in the family. Neil assumed most of the responsibility for the dog's care, and the dog rewarded these efforts with attention and love. When Neil felt lonely he would curl up with his dog and talk to it. Neil described how comforting the dog's presence was, and how he always felt better after he had talked with his friend.

The middle child, particularly, may experience more lonely feelings than other children (see "How a Pet Can Help With Sibling Rivalry"). He or she sees the oldest child getting special privileges and more attention. (By the time the second child reaches milestones, they are no longer so exciting.) And the youngest child seems special because, well, he or she is the last one. In addition, by this time, the parents feel more comfortable with themselves and may tend to relax those strict rules the older children had to obey. The middle child needs special attention, and a new pet may be the answer. After all, a dog or cat or rabbit will not compare the middle child to siblings, as parents and teachers tend to do. And if love is given, it surely will be returned.

Boredom often is an adjunct to loneliness. The best way to avoid this is to encourage your child to get involved with a new hobby or activity. A pet can cure this problem easily. Your child can feed, groom, exercise, and train it. Certainly the pet's presence can obliterate both boredom and loneliness.

DISCIPLINARY PROBLEMS; A PET CAN HELP

Discipline is training or experience that corrects, molds, and strengthens. The purpose of discipline is to teach a sense of inner regulation, thereby increasing one's feeling of self-esteem. Parents put limits on children, hoping the child will learn how to instill his or her own limits as he or she matures. But sometimes the child resists these parental efforts, and a disciplinary problem results. Psychologist Thomas Gordon, in his Parent Effectiveness Training, recommends a problem-solving approach to disciplinary problems. He suggests the family first identify and clarify the problem. Empathetic listening by the parents is a necessity. The family must then work together to come to a democratic solution. Allowing the child a voice in the rules and regulations is a better approach than simply "laying down the law" (*P.E.T.: Parent Effectiveness Training; The Tested New Way to Raise Responsible Children* [New York: P. H. Wyden, 1972]).

Kyle, ten, and his mother, Terry, entered therapy after Kyle had already developed a reputation at school for being a troublemaker. His constant interruptions in the classroom and his refusal to accept direction from any authority were affecting his achievement and his social adjustment. And, at home, no matter how Terry phrased her demands (gently, loudly, or tearfully), he refused them: he would not clean up his room, finish his homework, or do his chores; he still got into fights; and he continued to come home with low marks in citizenship. I learned that Kyle's parents had divorced when the boy was seven. His mother had been concerned about being a single parent and worried that her methods of child rearing were not succeeding. Therefore, she had gone through a period when she had been too lenient with the boy. Now that she had decided to toughen her approach to him, he was resisting. After talking to both of them, I could see that some of Kyle's behavior was caused by a need for attention. In addition, I could see that Terry's limit setting had become an ongoing power

struggle between the two: Terry set up a rule and Kyle opposed it. First I addressed the issue of Kyle's anger over his parents' divorce. When that issue was settled, his mother and I were
ready to make some changes in his disciplinary problems. The
first thing we did was involve him in making the rules. A clear
structure was set up, so that both he and his mother would know
when he was following the mutually set goals. Now we needed
motivation, which is the first step to success with any goal. Because
Kyle was eager to have a dog, we used the pet as his motivation.
Kyle helped to design his version of the petition for pet ownership
and care, and he became actively involved in the selection and care
of his new dog. The introduction of the pet into the household, the
contract, and the active interest that Kyle took in caring for his pet
started the boy on the road to self-discipline. He never shirked his
duties, he learned to care for something else, he received much
needed attention, and his self-esteem rose tremendously. Both
Kyle and Terry learned to listen to each other's viewpoints. He no
longer had problems with authority figures. Even his marks in
school improved.

The Benefits of Dog Obedience Training in Dealing With Disciplinary Problems

Having a school-age child be responsible for training the family pet
has a twofold benefit: the dog becomes trained, and the child
attains a new respect for the benefits of discipline. As a result, the
child's own sense of self-discipline and concentration become
more pronounced. And if a parent (or expectant parent) attends a
dog obedience class, he or she will learn to be firm and consistent
with his or her children. In fact, many of the principles of dog
obedience training are taken from human psychological learning
theories. At obedience school one learns to set limits, to reinforce
good behavior with praise, and to motivate with affection, attention, and interest. After all, there is no arguing with a dog: it's
either yes or no, good or bad! If you neglect to keep up with the
techniques taught in class, you quickly discover that the dog does
not obey. The same is true with your child. A parent who is too
permissive does not contribute to a child's sense of security. Once
realistic expectations have been set for a child, it is important for
the parents to follow through with a consistent program of train-

ing. Good training — whether it's with a child or an animal — lets your subject know exactly what you expect, with consistency and love.

IS YOUR CHILD SHY?

Research suggests that shy parents are more likely to have shy offspring. Yet shyness can also be caused by experiences away from home, say, with teachers or classmates. Psychologist Philip Zimbardo of the Stanford Shyness Clinic reports that shy children dislike being by themselves and tend to be dependent on others for entertainment and for alleviation of boredom. Studies at Zimbardo's clinic also show that shy children are less talkative, more unassertive, more submissive, more anxious, more distrustful of others; they are more prone to feel guilt and are less skilled in social situations (Philip G. Zimbardo and Shirley L. Radl, *The Shy Child: A Parent's Guide to Overcoming and Preventing Shyness from Infancy to Adulthood* [Garden City, N.Y.: Doubleday & Co., Dolphin Books, 1982]). Shyness tends to go hand in hand with low self-esteem. A self-critical child wants to avoid social situations and is overly concerned about evaluation from others. This child is often afraid of new people and anticipates criticism or failure when put in a new situation. As a result he or she avoids getting close to others or making new friends. Parents should take a look at the social model represented to their child (whether it's one of them or is some other person or situation) and with this evaluation, they can help their child overcome shyness.

Shirley, eight, had always been a quiet child, looking up to her two outgoing, athletic older brothers. Although she admired and loved them, she was completely overshadowed by them. She came to me for therapy after her family had moved to a new neighborhood. Her problem with shyness had been exacerbated by the change and by all the new experiences. Finally, she had not been able to manage all the changes and had become even more shy and withdrawn. In my talks with Shirley, she described to me her relationships with her cat and dog. I noticed that her sense of confidence and her ability to express herself were much better when she talked about her animals. I suggested to Shirley's mother that a stage be set up in the backyard, where Shirley could act out a play about her new school. Shirley could play herself and her pets could play the parts of different classmates. Shirley set up props to create a classroom and a playground. She even dressed up the animals! During this playacting process and with the love of her pets as a foundation, Shirley was able to interact with her "classmates" in a relaxed way; finally, she was learning some much needed social skills.

Shyness in a younger child may occur when he or she has not yet learned appropriate social skills. In Shirley's case she had never learned how to make friends because she had relied on her brothers to do it for her. To change shy behavior, a child can rehearse different ways of relating to new children or teachers by practicing with an accepting audience (siblings, parents, pets, and so on). A pet is a good subject of such a practice session because it won't tease or get impatient or talk back. A shy child is unaware of how his or her body gives out a message that says, Don't approach me.

Helping Your Child Develop Social Skills

A pet is particularly helpful when a child is trying to change body language. A child can touch the pet, and give it friendly pats or hugs. Following are some social skills your child can rehearse with a pet.

1. Practice sharing a secret.

2. Try giving praise.

3. Attempt to be a good listener.

4. Think of interesting things to say.

5. Practice making direct eye contact.

6. Make a conscious effort to smile.

In teaching a child independence, there are a few basics to consider. For instance, the child should be encouraged to do specific things such as going for a walk, reading a book, or taking care of a pet. The shy child needs to have a focus outside of his or her feelings of insecurity and self-criticism. Bringing a pet into the family is a way to teach a child independence. By taking care of and enjoying the pet, a child is rewarded with a feeling of confidence and self-acceptance. Encouraging a child to participate in obedience training a dog, for example, will promote a feeling of self-esteem, which in turn cultivates an outgoing, extroverted spirit.

Guidelines for Helping the Shy Child

Here are some suggestions for parents who want to help their shy child.

1. Encourage your child to stand up for himself or herself. Don't jump in too quickly to defend your child to a sibling or young friend.

2. Set up activities with which your child is likely to have success. Encourage your child to approach each activity one step at a time. (Dog obedience training is an excellent example of this type of progressive success.)

3. Encourage your child to try new situations, no matter the risk, and praise him or her for trying, no matter the result.

4. Do not reward shy behavior.

5. Listen to your child; encourage him or her to put thoughts and feelings into words.

6. Don't be afraid to call on your pet for help. Encourage your child to play, be silly, and enjoy physical freedom with the family pet. The animal will be a model of loose, natural, outgoing behavior for your child.

7. Keep your expectations in check. Be familiar with age-appropriate behavior, so you do not expect more of your child than he or she is capable of doing.

IF YOUR CHILD STUTTERS

Stuttering, if it occurs, usually starts between the ages of two and three, when children begin to master their verbal skills. The parents may be concerned about this problem, but they should not correct the child; instead, they should ignore the repetition of sounds. There is some evidence suggesting that a child who ordinarily stutters will not do so while in the presence of a pet. The animal gives the child a sense of confidence and relaxation.

If the stuttering continues as your child gets older, you should evaluate the expectations you have of your child; they may be too high. This is an excellent time to introduce a pet. Encourage your child to take on the parenting role of the animal; have your child aid in the animal's "social" skills (promote neighborhood walks, for instance). Encourage your child to play and talk with the family pet so he or she can experience the success of an uninhibited conversation. (Educators have long known that promoting learning through play motivates the child and encourages success.) As the child hears himself or herself conversing using appropriate speech patterns, he or she will learn to relax and will transfer the animal's acceptance and stability to his or her own sense of self-esteem. The majority of stuttering children outgrow this handicap if it is treated with kindness and patience.

SURVIVING ADOLESCENCE

The foundation for the adolescent's self-esteem has been laid before he or she reaches the teenage years, but he or she still needs the time to explore the senses, to achieve independence from parents, to establish significant relationships with peers, and to strive for acceptance. Certainly this is a stressful time for the teenager and his or her family. As parents who have lived through their children's adolescence know, this is a period of great unpredictability. During the course of a day, a teenager's mood can swing from a childlike dependency on the parents to a sudden demand for more freedom; he or she can be joyous one minute and in the depths of despair the next. When life does not treat the teenager fairly, the parents almost always get the blame.

The need to be popular is a major adolescent concern. The fear of rejection — the horror of being different — weighs heavily on the teenager. Teenagers need to express their feelings. Oftentimes the parent moves forward to offer support, but this is the moment when the adolescent has decided to take a stand for independence, and so rejects the parent as confidante. Some adults have an especially hard time understanding and being sympathetic to adolescent rebellion. The parent may react by withdrawing or feeling otherwise discouraged. The teen's peer group may reject him or her in some arbitrary or cruel manner. But the pet is always there.

Adolescents often have difficulty showing their affection to others. During this stage the teenager may consider it silly or embarrassing to express affection to family members. But cuddling with a pet is more acceptable. He or she can maintain a feeling of independence while expressing a need for love.

As we have seen thus far, pets offer much support to children; a pet would be especially useful during the adolescent period, when emotions run high. Animals offer love, companionship, and the opportunity to prove responsibility as the child moves through this tumultuous period on the way to adulthood.

Lexi, fourteen, had felt sad, angry, and rejected when her father had left her mother. After the divorce her mother had returned to work, leaving Lexi feeling angry at, and rejected by, both her mother and father. Soon Lexi had begun staying out late on weekend nights. Her mother had patiently tried to talk to her daughter about this new, unacceptable habit, but Lexi had felt guilty for being angry with her mother and she had refused to reveal her feelings. In fact, when she started therapy, Lexi wasn't able to express her feelings at all. After about three months she began to open up a little. At this time I thought a journal might be a way Lexi could express her feelings. She liked the idea of keeping a record of her private thoughts and personal expressions, but didn't have the discipline to keep a regular record. Then I suggested that she use her springer spaniel in her attempt to track her feelings. I recommended that the two go to a private place at the same time each day. Then Lexi could talk to the dog about whatever was on her mind. Because the dog never asked questions or reprimanded her, Lexi felt comfortable enough to speak freely. Eventually, Lexi's therapy with me and with the spaniel gave her enough confidence to face her parents and express her disappointment over their divorce. She even found she could separate her life from her parents' failed marriage. And her union with her pet was so tight and her home life so much more comfortable that she began to prefer staying home on weekends, thus solving her disciplinary problems.

Another patient, Jamie, sixteen, was much more of a disciplinary problem than Lexi. His grades had been slipping to below
average, yet he had rejected every suggestion his parents had
made for improving them. He had quit his high school football
team and had begun to spend more time with boys his parents
considered undesirable. Certainly his hopes for a college career
had been dwindling. The family had tried to chalk it up to adolescence, but finally the family had found itself in a vicious circle: the
more the parents had criticized, the more Jamie had avoided his
homework; the worse his grades had gotten, the lower his self-
esteem had dropped, and the more he had searched for acceptance
from his unsavory friends. Both he and his family had lost confidence in Jamie's ability to make decisions about what was best for
him. When I first began to work with the family, the members were
unable to express themselves clearly; they were at a terrible
impasse. Finally, with time, they opened up and could more freely
describe their feelings. By that time Jamie had become such a
disciplinary problem that his parents had restricted most of the
boy's privileges. So the parents needed to allow Jamie the freedom
to work on his problem. He mentioned to me that he liked dogs,
and was especially close to his own collie. He and I thought of a
way he could utilize his affection for the four-legged creatures to
gain a sense of responsibility, thus raising his self-esteem. He
decided to start a neighborhood grooming business. It was a good
solution, for the boy's disciplinary problems evaporated as his
sense of self-worth increased. His parents learned to allow him
more freedom, and he used this constructive way to assert his
independence.

Getting Past Adolescence

Despite the adolescent's demands for privacy and attempts to
ignore parental support, there are things that parents can do to
help their offspring during this transitional period. Here are some
guidelines.

1. If you have the opportunity to listen to your teenager's
problem, *don't give advice.*

2. Listen to what is being said without being judgmental.

3. Let your teenager know that you believe in his or her ability to solve the problem, and that you have confidence in his or her judgment.

4. Share some of your adolescent experiences with your teenager.

5. Respect your teenager's privacy with regard to his or her room, phone conversations, journals, or confidences told to a pet.

6. Be aware of his or her sensitivity to appearance and physical change.

7. Don't criticize your teenager's friends.

8. If your teenager feels rejected by peers, focus on his or her individuality. Avoid comparisons.

9. Encourage a relationship with the family pet, who can serve as confidante and loving counselor during this period of stress and change.

Adolescence can be survived! Keep these guidelines in mind, and hold onto your sense of humor. Above all, remember that this is just another developmental period, and it too, will pass.

SUMMARY

Animals provide a vital resource for the healthy development of children. They offer different roles of support for the child as he or she passes through each stage of development. For example, a pet can aid your toddler in physical development. The animal's non-judgmental acceptance enhances self-esteem. Later on, taking care of the pet teaches responsibility and fosters self-discipline. Companionship is always available. If your child has a problem (loneliness, shyness, and so on), a pet can offer the empathetic love your child needs. Certainly the task of parenting a happy child is made easier with the help of the family pet.

CHAPTER SIX

Serving Human Needs With Animals

A nimals have served the needs of their human companions for thousands of years. The ancient Greeks believed that dogs' tongues possessed medicinal qualities, and so used them to lick the wounds of the sick on their shrine at Epidaurus. This conviction about animals' importance to humans has evolved to such a degree that medical and educational communities have researched and developed pet-facilitated therapy. Today animals are commonly used in the care and treatment of certain groups, such as the homebound or institutionalized elderly, hospital patients, and the physically, mentally, or emotionally handicapped.

In 1792, England's York retreat was the first facility to formally use animals in treatment. Animals were part of the living environment, and the patients were encouraged to take care of them. This was the first case of humans using pets to change the behavior of the mentally ill. In 1867 epileptics were helped at the Bethel treatment facility in Germany by living with farm animals and among wildlife. The first use of therapy with animals in America was at Pawling Army Air Corps Convalescent Hospital in New York in 1942. The veterans who were recovering from physical injury and emotional trauma were encouraged to work with farm animals and to study reptiles and local wildlife. Turtle races and frog-jumping contests were organized as a form of recreational therapy (Leo K. Bustad, *Animals, Aging, and the Aged,* University of Minnesota Press, Minneapolis, 1980).

In 1953 psychologist Boris M. Levinson discovered that his shaggy dog, Jingles, could act as a cotherapist in diagnosing and treating the emotional problems of his patients both old and young. (*Pet-Oriented Child Psychotherapy* [Springfield, Ill.: Charles C. Thomas, 1972]). In the 1970s hospital psychologists Samuel A. Corson and Elizabeth O'Leary Corson found that adolescent patients in their care showed impressive improvement when dogs were introduced into their ward (Samuel A. Corson and Elizabeth O'Leary Corson, "Pet Dogs as Nonverbal Communication Links in Hospital Psychiatry,"*Comprehensive Psychiatry,* vol. 18, no. 1 [Jan. – Feb. 1977]). Encouraged by further research concerning dogs in therapy, the Corsons extended their work to nursing home residents (Samuel A. Corson and Elizabeth O'Leary Corson, "The Socializing Role of Pet Animals in Nursing Homes: An Experiment in Nonverbal Communication Therapy," in *Proceedings of the International Symposium on Society, Stress and Disease: Aging and Old Age,* June 14–19, 1976 [N.Y.: Oxford University Press, n.d.]). They found that the animals promoted self-reliance and increased the patients' social abilities. During this same period a book was published by Elizabeth Yates describing a program at Children's Psychiatric Hospital in Michigan, in which an orphan dog's presence on the children's ward helped some disturbed youngsters find their way back to health (*Skeezer: Dog with a Mission* [Irvington-On-Hudson, N.Y.: Harvey House, 1973]).

Today the medical community, including psychologists and physical therapists, is joining with animal organizations and community volunteers to help bring animals to special populations.

ANIMAL THERAPY
FOR THE ELDERLY

The elderly have special needs, and pets can help meet their needs. Pets can be talked to and can serve as the center of conversations with friends and family. A pet can help satisfy the elderly person's tactile needs as well. (Tactile needs usually increase with age, because other senses often are reduced. Living alone and dealing with the loss of family members or close friends also can cause an increase in the need for touching.) And at a time when the elderly may feel that their usefulness has declined, animals give them a feeling of being needed. Also, although friends and family may not spend much time with older people, animals do not discriminate against the elderly; they are friendly to anyone who shows them affection. In addition, dogs provide a sense of safety and an incentive for regular exercise. Pets also serve as a link to younger, perhaps more carefree, years.

Other pets, such as birds and fish, also provide pleasure and companionship for the elderly. In 1974 British researchers Roger Mugford and J. G. M'Comisky studied a group of elderly persons who lived alone. They divided them into three groups: one group received a visit from a social worker, along with a begonia plant; one received a visit from a social worker, who gave group members a parakeet; the last group received only a visit from a social worker. Questionnaires and observations revealed that those who had been given parakeets stopped talking about their own difficulties and began talking about their new pets. There was a significant improvement in self-esteem and an increase in all-around happiness ("Some Recent Work on the Psychotherapeutic Value of Caged Birds with Old People," in Pet Animals and Society, ed. R. S. Anderson [London: Bailliere Tindall, 1975]).

Research shows that 90 percent of the elderly live in their own homes or apartments. According to Daniel Lago, Ph.D., who heads the Gerontology Center at Pennsylvania State University, and Barbara Knight, M.P.S.S., future generations of elderly persons will remain at home for as long as possible, having services delivered to them, rather than opting for institutional care ("Companion Animals for the Elderly," in Dynamic Relationships in Practice: Animals in the Helping Professions, ed. Phil Arkow [Alameda, Calif.: The Latham Foundation, 1984]).

And, according to a 1986 study by Sharon E. Bolin, R.N., Ed.D., dean at West Suburban College in Oak Park, Illinois, a pet provides a source of support following the death of a spouse. She interviewed eighty-nine women who had recently lost their husbands. She found that pets significantly eased the pain of loss for the widows, and that non–pet owners were more anxious and concerned about their own deaths than were those who owned pets (Sharon E. Bolin, "Effects of Companion Animals During Conjugal Bereavement," paper presented at the Delta Society International Conference, Living Together: People, Animals, and the Environment, Boston, August 20–23, 1986).

Pet ownership, however, does have its difficulties. One problem for senior citizens who wish to maintain a pet at home is finding rental housing. One hopeful sign is that federal laws (and some state laws) have addressed this problem, and since 1983 pets have been permitted in federal government housing for the elderly. As mentioned in Chapter One, in a study reported by Lynette A. Hart, Ph.D., of the School of Veterinary Medicine, University of California at Davis, results show that pets in such governmentally assisted housing did not create problems with regard to noise, personal injury, or property damage. And interviews with property managers indicated that senior residents were responsible pet owners who benefited from pet ownership by developing positive mental attitudes, maintaining regular exercise routines, and feeling more secure. Results of this study should help to encourage local housing authorities to support the idea of pets and the elderly living together (Lynette A. Hart, "Effects of Pets in California Public Housing for Elderly: Perspectives of Residents and On-Site Managers," paper presented at the Delta Society International Conference, Living Together: People, Animals, and the Environment, Boston, August 20–23, 1986).

Organizations That Promote
A Bond Between Pets and the Elderly

An example of a community program that is successful in bringing the elderly and animals together is PACT (People and Animals Coming Together). This Pennsylvania State University volunteer group matches homeless animals with senior citizens. But PACT does more than place animals in the homes of the elderly. A volunteer interviews each person who requests a pet and then carefully matches an animal with that person's needs and abilities. Local veterinarians examine each animal, free of charge, to ascertain its health before it is placed. Finally, the animal spends at least one week in the home of a PACT volunteer in order to make sure it has a good temperament and is properly trained. In addition, PACT provides a sponsor for each owner–pet pairing. This sponsor helps train the pet, takes it to the veterinarian, and may perform tasks, such as bathing or grooming, that older people might find physically difficult. The organization agrees to take the pet back if the owner becomes ill or if the two aren't compatible.

Another organization that enhances the relationship between pets and the elderly is the Pets Are Wonderful Council (PAW), a nonprofit group based in Chicago. This program matches young people with older adults who need help caring for their pets. Paw Pals are youngsters who have completed a Boy Scout, Girl Scout, or 4-H pet care program, and who know how to give proper care to dogs and cats. Paw Pals are matched to adults in their community, and they offer to walk, groom, or feed their pets. Pet care sheets are provided so the youngsters can keep careful records of their pet care duties. This program is an ideal way, through the use of pets, to bridge the generation gap between young and old.

Veterinary and humane associations across the nation also sponsor the placement and care of orphan cats and dogs with senior citizens. CATS (Children and Animals Together for Seniors), a program in New York, gives animals (strays from local shelters) to the elderly. The new pet owners are provided with free pet food and other free services for pets, such as medical care and equipment. In addition, children who volunteer to receive instruction in pet care become the animals' walkers and groomers. The San Francisco Society for the Prevention of Cruelty to Animals (SPCA) conducts a program that furnishes pet food to Meals on Wheels, a home, health, and hospice service that delivers food to the elderly. Another program for the homebound elderly is Pet-A-Pet, in El Paso, Texas. This group supplies food and veterinary services to their clients.

Information about these and other animal programs for the elderly are available from the Delta Society, an international organization devoted to promoting the bond between people and pets. (See Appendix A for further information.)

NURSING HOME THERAPISTS

In conjunction with my work in pet therapy, I decided to visit a convalescent home with my dog Lorelei. I chose Lorelei over my other dog and two cats because she was the older of my two Rottweilers, and her age and four years of experience as my pet therapist had given her a mellow personality and a calm temperament. Before our first visit, she had to be checked by her vet. Her shots were up to date, her health was excellent, and no evidence of internal parasites was found. We were ready! Lorelei and I were then trained by Floriana Strahl, a volunteer from Animal Alliance in Los Angeles. This pet group sends loving, well-trained dogs to local nursing homes for weekly visits.

After checking in with the head nurse on each floor, Floriana showed us which residents enjoyed pet visits. Lorelei and I were greeted enthusiastically. Floriana and I listened to dog stories as Lorelei received many strokes and much attention. Our tour ended in the recreation room, where a number of the elderly shared stories about their own animals. We took photographs of Lorelei with some of her new friends and sent them to the residents when they were developed. I could tell from the smiles and comments that the residents appreciated her visit. She enjoyed their attention as much as they appreciated her affection. The recreation director told me that she was working on a project to bring in a permanent pet therapist.

Operators of nursing homes, convalescent centers, and retirement homes are beginning to understand the therapeutic value of pets. The pioneering work of psychologists Samuel Corson and Elizabeth O'Leary Corson with nursing home residents illustrates the impact that dogs have on the elderly in nursing homes. In their study the Corsons found that dogs in a nursing home offered love and tactile reassurance, and that their childlike play reduced stress and was rejuvenating. They discovered that friendly and sociable dogs offered a more positive nonverbal message than even the most well-intentioned nursing home staff member. Not only did the dogs succeed in bringing depressed elderly patients out of their shells, but they encouraged conversation between patients, diverting them from their worries and ills (Samuel A. Corson and Elizabeth O'Leary Corson, "Companion Animals as Bonding Catalysts," in *Geriatric Institutions in Interrelationships Between People and Pets*, ed. Bruce Fogle (Springfield, Ill.: Charles C. Thomas, 1981).

Psychologist Clark Brickel studied nursing homes that allowed each ward a feline mascot, and found that patients were comforted by, and enjoyed stroking, the cats. Some patients didn't like the cats, but the animals knew instinctively to avoid those patients. Brickel found that the cats made the ward environment seem more like a home than an institution (Clark M. Brickel, "The Therapeutic

Roles of Cat Mascots with a Hospital-Based Geriatric Population: A Staff Survey,"*The Gerontologist*, vol. 19, no. 4 [1979]).

In 1981 research reported from the Caulfield Geriatric Hospital in Melbourne, Australia, showed that a single dog named Honey had a positive effect on the physical and mental health of its sixty patients. The dog's presence promoted laughter, alertness, and increased incentive for living. In fact, Honey received so much attention that she developed a weight problem and had to go on a diet (I. M. Salmon, R. S. Salmon, R. S. Hogarth-Scott, and R. B. Lavelle, "A Dog in Residence." A Companion–Animal Study commissioned by the Joint Advisory Committee on Pets in Society [JACOPIS], Australia).

Veterinarian Leo K. Bustad is co-founder of the People-Pet-Partnership in Pullman, Washington. Dr. Bustad, who is president of the Delta Society, has pioneered pet therapy in geriatric and institutional settings. In the article that he coauthored with Linda M. Hines, "Placements of Animals With the Elderly: Benefits and Strategies," they describe how animals serve the needs of the elderly. They discuss how pets restore order to the lives of older people, linking their owners to a community of caring people and loving animals (*Guidelines: Animals in Nursing Homes* Revised Edition [California Veterinary Medical Association, 1987]).

Adopting an animal into a nursing home can bridge the gap that the elderly often feel when they move from the familiarity of their homes to a strange new environment. As shown, pets provide a multitude of recreational activities and also opportunities for companionship. Feeding, walking, and talking to animals dispel some of the loneliness and isolation that the elderly can experience in an institution.

Introducing an Animal Therapist Into a Nursing Home

Randall Lockwood, Ph.D., of the Humane Society of the United States, in a Latham Foundation newsletter, discusses the need for guidelines and training for those involved with animals and the elderly ("Pet-Facilitated Therapy Grows Up," *The Latham Letter*, vol. 11, no. 3 [Summer 1986]). The key to a successful program is good planning. Supervision and the welfare of the animals require ongoing evaluation, and volunteers offering pet services need proper training. Such planning is especially important when placing a pet as a full-time resident in a nursing home. Preparing staff members and residents for the responsibility of pet ownership is important. Cappy McLeod, in her book *Animals in the Nursing Home: A Guide for Activity Directors,* offers invaluable information and guidelines. She discusses every need, from training volunteer animal handlers to planning a pet open house introduction for residents. She also lists recreational activity programs in which pets can be used. If you or your institution is implementing a pet adoption program, following these guidelines can prevent possible problems (Colorado Springs, Colo.: McLeod, 1982).

Help in setting up a nursing home pet program is also available in a book edited by journalist Phil Arkow called *The Loving Bond: Companion Animals in the Helping Professions* (R. & E. Publishers, California, 1987). Another excellent resource is *Guidelines: Animals in Nursing Homes,* available from the Delta Society. It describes how to evaluate nursing homes using pet programs and details the steps necessary for effective placement and follow-up of the animals chosen.

Programs That Sponsor Animal Visits to Nursing Homes

Some local humane societies offer another type of enriching experience for nursing home residents. Petmobiles bring cats and dogs to the nursing homes on a regular basis. These organizations can also encourage field trips to the shelters by the residents who wish to break their daily routines by playing with the shelter animals.

In the past few years, human service agencies have become involved with pet therapy programs for the elderly. Baltimore's Pets on Wheels, for example, organized in 1982, is sponsored by the city's Commission on Aging and Retirement Education. This group uses carefully trained volunteers to visit area nursing homes with equally trained pets.

Some governmental organizations are turning to professional pet therapy groups to provide service to nursing homes. In 1984, the Pennsylvania Society for the Prevention of Cruelty to Animals (SPCA) and the Pennsylvania Women's SPCA turned their pet therapy programs over to Pals for Life, a nonprofit organization that specializes in bringing visiting animals to more than fifty nursing homes and senior centers. Institutions that cannot afford to pay the group's minimal fee are supported by local businesses or by contributions from the United Way. Visiting pets are owned by the Pals for Life staff, and those animals that become nursing home residents are supervised and trained by the group's staff members.

Other programs across the country successfully involve the community in bringing animals and nursing home residents together. PALS, located in Boise, Idaho, has an educational program for young people who visit nursing home residents with their animals. Students from the Scouts organizations, 4-H clubs, and the YMCA attend training sessions that instruct youngsters on dealing with the physical limitations of the elderly. Companion Animal Partnership, a program at Washington State University, sponsors students and other volunteers, who take pets chosen largely from a pet-lending roster, to nursing homes for visits. This program also offers a petting zoo for children, and dog shows and obedience demonstrations on the grounds of nursing homes. (In fact, after one dog show, an orphan dog was adopted as a result of a prescription written by a nursing home resident's physician.) Therapy Dogs International, in Hillside, New Jersey, registers dogs whose owners take them to visit the elderly and the emotionally disabled. Membership is open to dog owners as well as to animal lovers in the community.

As the need for, and use of, animal therapists for the elderly increases, research and community involvement will continue. Guidelines and suggestions for people who wish to start such a program or organization are available from the Delta Society. The group also maintains a computer file of the programs already in existence (see Appendix A). Dedication and planning are needed as these four-footed therapists reach out to bring joy to the elderly.

HELPING THE HANDICAPPED

Guide Dogs for the Blind

Probably the best-known animal service for the handicapped is guide dogs for the blind. During World War I dogs were trained as messengers and guides for rescue work. Following the war the Germans trained dogs to help their blinded veterans and civilians. It was found that guide dogs offered the blind the opportunity to lead independent lives. Currently, training facilities are established throughout the world.

The first Seeing Eye guide dog center in the United States was established in 1929 by Dorothy Harrison Eustis, a German shepherd breeder. There are now eleven guide dog training centers in the United States. They vary in methodology, funding, and selection of dogs. Most schools charge little or no fee to the guide dog recipient, depending instead on private funding.

Training of instructors and guide dogs is not taken lightly. For instance, California has a state law requiring guide dog instructors to complete a three-year apprenticeship at a guide dog school. Then they must pass a state board examination. In training the dogs the instructors learn to simulate blindness by using blindfolds while walking their dogs on suburban and city streets. Dogs require nearly forty of these walking tours before they are ready to begin instruction with a blind person.

Guide Dogs for the Blind in San Rafael, California, offers an in-residence training program. They breed their own German shepherds, Labrador retrievers, and golden retrievers. These dogs are selected for their willingness to work, even temperaments, ease of grooming, and size. A puppy is observed and tested for three months. Then it is placed in a foster home with a 4-H member to assure normal socialization. At eighteen months the dog is returned to the school for guide dog training and eventual bonding with its new blind owner. The new owner receives a four-week training course with his or her dog companion and then an extensive period of follow-up training. The working life of a guide dog is normally between eight and ten years. A retired dog may stay on with the blind owner as a pet, or it may be returned to the family that raised it. A new dog is then brought in, and the owner goes into a new training period with his or her new guide.

In opting to use a guide dog, the blind person makes a life choice that affects more than his or her mobility. A guide dog offers the blind person physical, social, and psychological benefits. Studies show that blind people who have dogs feel safer, have increased physical confidence and stamina, and have greater self-esteem. The relationship developed with the animal offers the blind person a feeling of self-respect in that the dog shows no judgment about his or her disability. In addition, the dog owner is more comfortable relying on the dog than he or she is asking for the same help from a person. The ability of the dog and owner to communicate verbally and nonverbally offers the owner emotional satisfaction and stability. The dog, then, not only is a trusted companion but is also a four-footed therapist.

See Appendix B for a list of guide dog programs.

Ears for the Deaf

There are three times as many deaf people as there are blind people in the United States. Just as Seeing Eye dogs are taught to provide "eyes" to the blind, Hearing Ear dogs provide "ears" to the deaf. Trained to listen for and to assist the hearing-impaired, these dogs alert their owners to specific sounds in their environments. There is no cost to the recipient for a Hearing Ear dog.

If a baby cries, for instance, the dog is trained to alert the deaf mother or father. Or when an alarm clock rings, the dog jumps up to wake the owner. A Hearing Ear dog can also be trained to alert its owner to sirens while the owner is driving, or to smoke alarms. Some dogs are taught to respond to the ringing of the telephone. Each sound triggers a different behavior: with the doorbell, the dog runs back and forth between the owner and the door; in the case of a smoke alarm, the dog drops to the ground in front of the owner to signal the emergency.

In 1975 Agnes McGrath, founder of International Hearing Dogs, Inc., became the first person to train dogs for the deaf in a program started by the Minnesota Society for the Prevention of Cruelty to Animals. Since that time training centers all over the United States, using animals from humane societies, have been placing Hearing Ear dogs with deaf owners.

The Hearing Ear Dog Program at West Boylston, Massachusetts, founded in 1976, is one of the many training centers in this country. The dogs, which are selected from animal shelters, must be healthy, intelligent, eager to please, and curious about sound. The dogs receive four to six months of training, depending on the number of sounds they will need to recognize. Before placement the new owner receives instruction in the care of the dog. The trainer explains and demonstrates the dog's abilities. Then dog and owner attend a two-week training program together. The owner is taught how to work with the dog and how to use obedience commands to control the animal. Because many of the deaf cannot speak clearly, the dog is taught to obey hand signals rather than verbal commands. When the dogs graduate, they receive a bright orange harness to identify them as Hearing Ear dogs. Follow-up help is available after the dog moves into its new home.

Another program is International Hearing Dog, Inc., in Henderson, Colorado. This group, organized in 1979, trains and places dogs in this country and Canada. Support for the program comes from community groups, most notably Silent Partners, which recruits sponsors for the training of individual dogs for the deaf. Sponsors receive a picture of the Hearing Ear dog, help in naming the animal, receive progress reports on the dog, and finally, receive news of the dog's new home.

Red Acre Farm, established in 1903, was once a location for Boston's retired city work horses. It began its hearing dog program in 1981 as a regional center for the American Humane Association. The dogs are orphans from shelters and go through four to six months of training in basic obedience and presence of sound. After undergoing an interview, owners are selected and matched with available dogs. Most of the clients are either completely deaf or have a profound hearing loss; some live alone or with a deaf spouse. After the trained dog is brought to the new home, a staff member supervises the dog–human team through the transition.

Dogs for the deaf are more than service dogs. They give love and security to their owners. They become members of the family. Based on a relationship of mutual affection, these four-footed therapists, like their counterparts for the blind, bring a new sense of independence into a soundless existence.

A list of training centers for Hearing Ear dogs is available from the Delta Society or the Latham Foundation (see Appendix A). (See also Appendix B for such a list.)

Dogs Who Help the Physically Handicapped

Service dogs are also available to help the physically handicapped. Service dogs aid those who are physically limited as a result of an accident, polio, cerebral palsy, muscular dystrophy, or some other disabling condition. These animal partners offer love and assistance to those who formerly lived an isolated, and restricted life. People who heretofore had been forced to depend on others can now rely on their canine companions. They learn to become more mobile and as a result have increased confidence. Physical obstacles are no longer as overwhelming. Dogs can be trained to open doors and to negotiate stairways. They also can be trained to pull wheelchairs up ramps and inclines. These dogs can learn to turn on lights, fetch and return items, push elevator buttons, carry supplies, pull grocery items off shelves, and even carry messages. For a physically impaired person, such a dog can save time and effort; he or she can then use his or her energy for more creative tasks, such as attending school or holding down a job.

Service dogs do more than overcome physical barriers for their owners. Physically handicapped people are susceptible to robbery or bodily attack. The service dog is trained to protect the owner, thus offering a needed sense of security. Their presence encourages conversation from strangers who might otherwise ignore or avoid the disabled person. Jane Eddy, M.S.W., at the California State University at Sacramento, reported in her research that disabled individuals with service dogs had five times more conversations with strangers than did those without dogs. In other words, the dog provided an opportunity for social contact; instead of seeing a person with a disability, the stranger saw someone with a working dog ("Service Dogs and Social Acknowledgement of People in Wheelchairs: An Observational Study," paper presented at the Delta Society International Conference, Living Together: People, Animals, and the Environment, Boston, August 20–23, 1986).

Physically impaired people are further empowered if they participate in dog obedience training. Competing at obedience shows allows them to feel equal to the other dog owners. Controlling their pets gives them a sense of competency and can also be a way for them to learn how to express their own needs. This form of self-assertion encourages self-esteem and pride; there is no need to rely on another person. Good dog training requires that the dog enjoy the learning; this gives the handicapped trainer an opportunity to renew an interest in learning. In addition, giving the dog commands can improve speech in brain-injured patients. The dog's acceptance of the commands encourages the owners to risk new speech patterns.

Bonita Bergin pioneered the program to use dogs for the physically and developmentally disabled. In 1975 this innovative special education teacher started Canine Companions for Independence. She had seen donkeys and burros carrying wares and assisting the disabled in Turkey. She believed that dogs could be trained to perform similar tasks. Her graduate studies in special education had convinced her that independence was what disabled persons needed and wanted most. The first Canine Companion dogs were raised and trained in her own backyard in Santa Rosa, California. By 1986 217 of these specially trained dogs had been placed all over the world. The dogs inspire the disabled to move out into the world as they receive help from their canine partners. Emotionally disturbed children begin to speak as their patient canine friends offer love and affection.

Originally, Canine Companion dogs assisted wheelchair users and people with mobility impairments. Now, Canine Companions also has signal dogs for the hearing-impaired, social dogs for pet therapy, and specialty dogs for seniors or people with multiple disabilities. These dogs learn as many as eighty-nine commands in order to help their disabled owners.

The dogs are selectively bred at Bergin's Santa Rosa facility. Potential working dogs are tested as puppies for their temperament. If they pass these tests, they are placed in private homes, where they learn socialization skills and basic commands in an environment of love and attention. Their foster parents, many of them teenagers, take them to local obedience classes. At about fifteen months, they are returned to the training facility for advanced training. When the dog graduates, the foster parent is invited to attend the ceremony and to meet the dog's new owner.

It costs approximately $5000 to train a Canine Companion dog. The nonprofit program is funded by private donations, membership, and service club contributions. Information about this program is available from Canine Companions for Independence, P.O. Box 446, Santa Rosa, California 95402.

Another nonprofit group offering help to the disabled is Handi-Dogs of Tucson, Arizona, founded by Alamo Reaves in 1974. This program teaches the disabled student to train his or her own dog rather than using a special teacher for that purpose. If the disabled participant does not own a dog, Handi-Dogs works with local dog breeders, the humane society, or animal welfare groups to locate a suitable animal. The dogs learn obedience training and special skills to help their owners: picking up dropped objects, fetching items, and barking on command. Volunteers, many former students themselves, help in this teaching program. Some of these dogs go on with their owners to compete successfully in obedience competition. Handi-Dogs also provides dogs for the deaf and the senior citizens of southern Arizona. A manual on dog training techniques for the disabled along with information on setting up a volunteer program is available from Handi-Dogs (see Appendix B).

A service dog can mean a whole new way of life for the handicapped. The activities that able-bodied people take for granted now can be routine for the disabled also, with the help of a four-footed therapist.

See Appendix B for a list of dog training centers for the physically impaired.

THERAPEUTIC HORSEBACK RIDING

For the physically and mentally handicapped, horseback riding offers outdoor exercise, a pleasurable experience, — and good therapy. All over the world members of the disabled community are learning to ride high in the saddle. They are moving out of a limited world with the help of professional instructors and specially trained horses. It is treatment for both body and spirit.

Liz Hartel, a polio victim once confined to a wheelchair, was instrumental in bringing horseback riding to the attention of the handicapped. This Danish horsewoman did not want her illness to get in the way of her riding. She insisted on using horseback riding as part of her therapy, and as a result, learned to regain her strength and level of confidence. She competed in the 1952 Olympics and won a Silver Medal for Dressage.

In England the following year, Pony Riding for the Disabled became the first school to teach riding to the handicapped. In 1970 the Cheff Center for the Handicapped, in Augusta, Michigan, a riding center for disabled adults and children, was started by Lida McCowan. Today North American Riding for the Handicapped Association, in Chicago, teaches riding and also evaluates more than two hundred different programs in the United States and Canada.

For disabled children horseback riding can be an experiential learning process. Positive social relationships develop with instructors and with other children. According to special education research by Helen Seals Tuel, Ed.D., children who ride in special programs show improvement with speech and learning skills. The visually impaired learn a new sense of locomotion. Emotionally disturbed youngsters improve their self-image and learn how to be more independent. In addition, riding helps children break out of the failure syndrome ("An Extended Treatment of the Impact of Therapeutic Horseback Riding on the Physical and Psychological Well-Being of Children and Adults with Motor, Sensory, and Intellectual Impairments," Ph.D. diss., George Peabody College for Teachers of Vanderbilt University, 1985). The National Center for Therapeutic Riding in Washington, D.C., serves more than five hundred urban children annually; it is a model program for the use of horses as an educational tool.

Hippotherapy as an Aid for Motor Dysfunction

Hippotherapy ("treatment with the help of a horse") is one form of therapeutic riding that is used primarily for motor dysfunction disabilities. Barbara Glasow, R.P.T., of Winslow Therapeutic Riding Unlimited (Warwick, New York), Jan Spink, M.S., of EFT Services (Chesterfield, Missouri), and Beth Stanford, R.P.T., Throncroft Equestrian Center (Malvern, Pennsylvania), are leading practitioners of hippotherapy, riding therapy, and developmental vaulting.

Hippotherapy is part of a physical therapy program that uses the movement of the horse to help the treatment of the patient. In this therapy, the rider does not attempt to control the horse, and thus there is no need to know riding skills. The patient sits on the horse and accommodates, with automatic reactions, to the three-dimensional swing motions of the horse's back as it walks. The actual session on the horse lasts twenty to thirty minutes, but the emotional benefit begins as soon as the patient is introduced to the horse. The therapy helps improve the rider's circulation, muscle tone, equilibrium reactions, internal body functions, and breathing ability. The hippotherapy session includes a physical therapist, physician, and horse expert. The physical therapists find that improvement in postural control and trunk equilibrium reactions comes about more easily on the horse than in the clinic. Along with the physical benefit, the emotional bonding and communication between rider and horse helps children as well as adults expand their world while taking part in a positive psychological experience.

Training in hippotherapy techniques and therapeutic riding is available from Winslow Therapeutic Riding Unlimited. Since its inception in 1974, the program has helped more than 2000 disabled persons. Along with classic hippotherapy, other workshops are offered, including elements of Oriental martial arts, imagery, and right-brain learning. They have provided services for disabled persons ranging from two to sixty-four years of age, who have suffered from cerebral palsy, spina bifida, mental retardation, learning impairments, emotional disturbances, social maladjustments, or multiple physical handicaps.

Further information on hippotherapy training centers can be obtained from the Delta Society (see Appendix A) or North American Riding for the Handicapped Association, Inc., 111 E. Wacker Drive, Chicago, IL 60601, 312–644–6610.

Recreational Riding as Therapy

Recreational riding therapy is another form of therapeutic horseback riding, different from hippotherapy. Recreational riding therapy teaches riding skills, riding styles, and equestrian competition. This type of horseback riding is appropriate for all classes of the disabled, including the physically, mentally, and emotionally handicapped. In recreational riding therapy students learn not only riding skills but how to care for their horses. The riding team, which uses the riding experience as part of the overall learning and rehabilitation program, usually includes a psychologist, speech therapist, and special education teacher.

Horseback riding strengthens and tones muscles, improves posture and coordination, increases joint mobility, and promotes awareness of the body in space, in that a horse's movements require a physical response from the rider. The horse offers independence from a wheelchair and introduces a bond of affection with a living animal.

Emotionally and mentally handicapped youngsters who use riding as part of their treatment show remarkable gains during therapy. Usually, children with these disabilities have a short attention span and a low tolerance level for frustration. Learning to ride helps them develop concentration and self-control. They increase their ability to communicate as they learn to control and talk to their horse. Thus their feelings of accomplishment are enhanced.

Organizations That Offer
Therapeutic Horseback Riding

The Colorado Therapeutic Riding Center in Boulder has been helping disabled children and adults since 1980. The center works with more than one hundred students during the year, offering professional and volunteer help in performing recreational therapy, which includes work with a 4-H group and basketball on horseback. This particular program was researched and it was found that horseback riding was an effective method of therapy. The disabled riders enjoyed physical exercise and learned new skills. In addition, they learned to make friends with other students and with staff members (V. Marie Fox, R. Lawler, and Marvin Luttges, "Measurement Device for Therapeutic Horseback Riding," paper presented at the Delta Society International Conference, Interactions of People, Animals, and the Environment, Denver, October 4–6, 1985).

Another active riding group, founded in 1982, is the We Can Ride organization in Minnetonka, Minnesota. The group uses facilities and horses provided by the Hennepin County Home School, and in exchange, it trains the school's 14- to 18-year-old handicapped residents. The classes are conducted by specially trained instructors, who are assisted by volunteers. All riders begin with three volunteers, one to lead the horse and two who walk beside and support the rider. In 1984 eleven of the students participated in a competitive horse show sponsored by the Therapeutic Equestrian Association of Minnesota (TEAM), the Special Olympics, and the Cerebral Palsy Association. These eleven riders brought back nineteen ribbons! We Can Ride offers scholarships when needed and has served more than sixty handicapped persons, ranging in age from four-and-a-half to sixty-seven.

Another riding program that offers an opportunity for the handicapped to learn riding skills is the Therapeutic and Recreational Riding Center in Lisbon, Maryland. In this program youngsters learn to ride and also how to groom, tack, and lead a horse properly. In addition, they become aware of safety and courtesy. This program is supported by volunteers and through community efforts.

Approximately 350 private, nonprofit groups offer some form of horseback riding therapy to handicapped children and adults. Funding usually comes from private and community sources.

Extra support is provided by the United Professional Horsemen's Association, the Morgan Horse Association, and the American Quarter Horse Association. In addition, members of the Pony Club and 4-H groups around the country volunteer their time.

The National Association of Sports for Cerebral Palsy, founded in 1976, offers those afflicted with cerebral palsy or related conditions a chance to engage in competitive sport. Physically disabled riders are now able to meet the challenges of dressage, equitation, and handy rider competitions.

The riding experience for the handicapped offers something beyond physical therapy: it offers a bond of love between horse and rider. Sitting on a horse, quietly talking to it, and grooming it may be the first steps toward a feeling of accomplishment and self-esteem.

A list of programs in the United States and Canada and further information on riding for the handicapped are available from North American Riding for the Handicapped Association, Inc., 111 E. Wacker Drive, Chicago, IL 60601, 312–644–6610.

ANIMALS AS HOSPITAL VISITORS

Studies have shown that animals can help in the recovery of hospitalized patients. Bedside visits by pets reduce anxiety, blood pressure, and loneliness. Seeing and talking to pets in a hospital room motivates the patient, helps him or her fight depression, and promotes better cooperation with treatment (Jacquelyn McCurdy, "Pet Companionship Program in the Hospital Setting," paper presented at the Delta Society International Conference, Living Together: People, Animals, and the Environment, Boston, August 20–23, 1986); (Lynn John Anderson, "Development of Viable Human–Animal Bond Program in the U.S. Military," paper presented at the Delta Society International Conference, Living Together: People, Animals, and the Environment, Boston, August 20–23, 1986). More than twenty-five hospitals in the United States are evaluating or are already using pet therapy as part of their treatment programs.

One of the instigators of this type of program was Jacquelyn McCurdy, R.N., B.S.N., who works at Milwaukee's Columbia

Hospital. After seeing the success of animals in nursing homes, she initiated the Pet Companionship Program, which was the first in the country to allow patients in the acute care facility to receive bedside visits from their own pets. Of course, careful guidelines were set up with the hospital's infection control committee and the administrative staff. Now when a patient is admitted to the hospital, information about the pet program is found in the admission packet. Currently, all patients are eligible to request a visit from their pets, except for those who have a suppression of the immune system or who are postsurgical and have draining wounds. Columbia Hospital also considers requests for visits by pets other than dogs or cats, on an individual basis. In fact, their geriatric unit has a parakeet as resident pet!

How the Program Works

After patient and pet have been evaluated and visits approved, a pet visit is scheduled. A trained volunteer greets the visiting pet at the hospital entrance. A member of the patient's family must accompany the animal. A certificate of rabies shots must be shown. A brief exam then follows. If all is well, the pet, held in a crate, is brought into the hospital room. The pet may then leave the crate, but is kept on a leash during the visit. A sign on the door lets the hospital staff know that a pet is in the room. The visit ends with a picture-taking session with patient and pet.

Current Hospital Pet Programs

The Prescription Pet Program began at Children's Hospital in Denver, Colorado, in 1985. It was started by Fern Bechtel, director of volunteers at Children's Hospital, when she noticed her own temporarily paralyzed son's response to the family dog following months of hospitalization after a car accident. She and Jan Facinelli, D.V.M., started the program with the oncology unit. The model program has been so successful as a therapeutic aid that it has expanded to include the psychiatric and orthopedic units.

Only medically screened adult dogs are eligible for this program. Physician and parental consent is required before the visit. A trained volunteer takes his or her dog to the patient's hospital room, where the child may pet or hold the animal. The patient's nurse is present during the visit to assist and to supervise the volunteer. During all visits dogs wear "volunteer smocks" to prevent the spread of hair and dander.

Parents, staff members, and volunteers who have taken part in the program report positive results. In every unit where pets have been allowed, patients have exhibited a marked reduction in stress, anxiety, and withdrawal when visited by the animals.

A similar program, Furry Friends Foundation, was started at Children's Hospital in Stanford, California, by Judy A. Kell. Observation of the close relationship and love between her daughter, Jennifer, and her cat during the child's fight against cancer convinced Judy of the therapeutic value of interaction between children and animals. While Jennifer recovered at home, her cat, Tabatha, never left her side. This experience inspired Judy to create a program in which animals visit hospitalized children. In many instances the children had suppressed immune systems because of their illnesses or their treatments. Thus superior health of the animals was crucial. With the help of pediatrician Cecil Agee and veterinarian John Quick, animals and volunteers were recruited. Community support included funds from Morgan Hill Rotary Club and volunteers from the local 4-H group.

In January 1984 the first pets visited Children's Hospital. Volunteers escorted an English shepherd, an Airedale terrier, two cocker spaniels, an Irish setter, a guide dog for the blind, a cat, rabbits, and a rat. Since that time animal visitors have also included sheep, llamas, birds, and snakes.

The program, which has been rewarding for volunteers and recovering patients alike, has shown that animals can reach children in a way that people sometimes can't. Currently, a variety of animals are provided by breeders, 4-H groups, Future Farmers of America, wildlife groups, and zoos. The program has now expanded to include visiting and consulting with other San Francisco Bay Area hospitals, including several children's hospitals and specialized treatment centers.

Furry Friends Foundation is a nonprofit organization supported by volunteers and through private donations. For further information contact Judy A. Kell, P.O. Box 1593, Morgan Hill, California 95037.

Major Lynn John Anderson, D.V.M., M.S.W., reports that visiting pet therapists are being used successfully by the U.S. Military Health Services. An animal visitation program (in which cats and dogs are used) is part of the treatment at the United States Soldiers' and Airmen's Home in Washington, D.C. Dr. Anderson reports that the animal visitation program in the hospital's pediatrics department is very successful. Children enjoy seeing their own pets in the hospital. (One eight-year-old boy who was fearful about his upcoming open heart surgery was reassured after examining a scar on his own dog.) Facing the fears of surgery can be difficult for children. Having their four-footed therapists beside them at the hospital bridges the gap between the sometimes frightening atmosphere of the hospital and the safety of home. It is easier for them to say what they feel when their animals are nearby. The pets also encourage the children to reach out to staff members and to talk to other patients.

PET-FACILITATED THERAPY FOR EMOTIONALLY DISTURBED CHILDREN

Emotionally disturbed children often experience difficulty with relationships and confused communication. When they relate to animals, however, these inadequate feelings subside. In *Pet-Oriented Child Psychotherapy* (Springfield, Ill.: Charles C. Thomas, 1972), psychologist Boris Levinson describes the healing value of pets in the residential treatment of children. He found that a pet, in a loving way, can help teach a child to make decisions and to become responsible. Also the animal gives a rehabilitation treatment center a more homey atmosphere. For a child who may never have enjoyed carefree play, a pet provides an opportunity to regress and to behave in a childlike manner. An animal will not betray confidences or break the trust of an already emotionally upset, mistrustful child. Introducing the child to dogs, cats, snakes, birds, and other animals allows him or her to feel good while experiencing a close, accepting relationship.

As mentioned, one of the first pet therapists to work with children was an affectionate dog, which, as described by Elizabeth Yates in her book *Skeezer: Dog With a Mission* (New York: Harvey House, 1973), helped the children in a mental hospital in Michigan. The children become calmer as they walked down the corridor and saw this dog, Skeezer, resting on the floor. The dog lived in the hospital in his own doghouse, and his presence helped the disturbed children develop a sense of family.

Rehabilitation ranch programs for disturbed and socially maladjusted children currently use farm animals to create a positive work experience. Taking care of the livestock and smaller animals gives the children, whose patterns of failure need to be turned around, a sense of direction and achievement. A working farm gives an urban child a chance to learn about a different way of life, and it gives him or her the opportunity to look after something other than himself or herself. The child learns to respect the animals' needs, which is a step toward respecting the rights of human beings.

Being with animals in an outdoor atmosphere also allows youngsters, who often are tense and anxious, a chance to express themselves verbally. The animals, who understand how to love the children without ambivalance, let them feel accepted. The dependency of the animal on the child gives the child a chance to feel important; thus a negative self-image begins to improve. The children begin to achieve goals, and then discover that they can enter 4-H competitions and win! For the child who has spent a lifetime looking at only the negative side of things, this can be a turning point. Feeding, cleaning, and parenting an animal gives the children a sense of pride. Instead of using their energy against others, they learn to work and to give love.

One of the many successful programs helping to change such youngsters is the George B. Page Boys Ranch in Ojai, California. The children work with the farm animals, which gives them a sense of achievement and enriches their educations. Dog obedience classes are also part of the program. Working with the animals increases the attention span of the hyperactive boys and redirects their energy. The presence of the animals also develops more positive relationships between the boys and the staff.

Emotionally disturbed children are often placed in residential care facilities. Whether the child is a preschooler or a teenager, he or she needs contact, acceptance, and love. Youngsters who are frightened and withdrawn will not or cannot put their feelings into words. Therapists and staff who use pets in the treatment of these disturbed children are learning that animals as cotherapists can help the children take firm steps on the difficult road to a positive reality.

ANIMALS WHO REHABILITATE IN PRISON

Animals have joined the working staffs of prisons and are performing well at improving morale among inmates. Pets-in-prison programs help prisoners, staff, and animal shelters and also provide a community resource. Learning how to work with animals offers the prisoner, who may be socially maladjusted, an opportunity to both feel acceptance and to engage in positive, productive activity.

One of the first prison pet programs was begun in 1975 at the Lima State Hospital for the Criminally Insane in Ohio, under psychiatric social worker Dave Lee. Three parakeets and an aquarium were introduced on one ward. The patients, most of whom were depressed and withdrawn, began to talk to, and involve themselves with, the pets. This was the beginning of the first successful pet therapy program in a maximum security mental hospital. By 1986, more than half of the wards at Lima were making use of 164 pets. The roster includes fish, rabbits, deer, goats, geese, macaws, parrots, hamsters, parakeets, ducks, and cats. The patients have learned to care for other living creatures, not just themselves. They have searched for insects for the birds, and learned to care for a pregnant guinea pig. They show interest and affection for the animals and a desire to help something else live. This has led to a prison-operated greenhouse, where tropical plants can be bartered for bird seed or rabbit food.

Research conducted at Lima showed success with the pet therapy. One of the studies compared a ward with pets to one without pets. The patients with pets required only half the medication, exhibited less violent behavior, and made no suicide attempts. (The ward without pets registered eight suicide attempts.) It was found that the pets helped the staff provide for the patients' needs. Small animals were especially helpful because of the close physical relationship between small pet and patient. (Some smaller animals, which offer comfort, are allowed to stay in the rooms during times of patient depression or isolation.) The animals gave the men an opportunity to turn attention away from themselves while learning how to provide a home for their pets. This often was the beginning of social or emotional change (Dave

Lee, "Companion Animals in Institutions," in *Dynamic Relation-ships in Practice: Animals in the Helping Professions,* ed. Phil Arkow [Alameda, Calif.: The Latham Foundation, 1984]).

Purdy Treatment Center for Women in Gig Harbor, Wash-ington, uses animals in its Prison Partnership program to pro-vide vocational training for inmates. The program is headed by trainers Don Jecs and Marsha Hinkle. Because of the success of prison programs in other institutions, prison officials in Washington were open to this innovative project that benefits both the prisoners and the rest of the community. Dogs that might otherwise have been destroyed are recruited for use in reeducat-ing inmates.

Inmates volunteer for the program and register for a class through the Tacoma Community College. The eleven-week course includes instruction in dog care and behavior; basic and advanced puppy and dog training; training dogs to assist the physically disabled, including the deaf; veterinary assistance; and kennel work.

A positive change in the women involved in the program is reported by prison staff members. The women must develop self-control and restraint, or they cannot remain in the program. They become more cooperative with all aspects of prison life and develop hope for the future. "Purdy dogs," as they are called by Leo Bustad, are changing life inside and outside prison walls.

The pet therapy program at Medium Security, District of Columbia Correctional Facility at Lorton, Virginia, was originated by veterinarian Earl Strimple. He had seen how a program called PAL (People – Animals – Love) had improved the quality of life for the elderly and the institutionalized. He started the PAL program at Lorton in 1982. The PAL club is composed of forty inmates who come together every Thursday night to learn about animal care. Forty small animals, such as birds, fish, rabbits, and guinea pigs, are kept at the facility, and veterinarian support, pet food, and pet care products are supplied. Members provide care for the animals and put out a newsletter about the club's activities. Loving the pets gives the inmates a chance to express positive feelings without a fear of rejection. The self-esteem of the men increases. The program is so successful, in fact, that there is a waiting list of inmates who want to join. Staff at Lorton are pleased with the inmates' progress and with the overall sense of responsibility that is being fostered through the use of the pet therapists.

The model for this innovative and well-planned program is available from the Delta Society (see Appendix A).

APPENDIX A

Resource Organizations

THE DELTA SOCIETY

The Delta Society, an international resource center that promotes the human–animal bond, was founded in 1976. This nonprofit service organization has more than 1000 members. They are veterinarians; educators; staff from animal service groups, nursing homes, hospitals, and other institutions; and animal lovers. Delta dispenses information and encouragement to pet-facilitated therapy programs around the world. Audiovisual aids and guidelines are made available to communities and institutions. The organization sponsors yearly conferences, which include scientific sessions and workshops. Delta publishes a membership magazine called *People – Animals – Environment*, along with a scientific journal, *Anthrozoös: A Multi-Disciplinary Journal on the Interactions of People, Animals, and the Environment*, which discusses findings regarding studies on human – animal interaction.

Leo K. Bustad, D.V.M., Ph.D., is president of Delta. He offers knowledge and inspiration to the organization's members. He helps programs around the world that wish to institute and nurture the human – animal bond. Linda M. Hines, M.A., is executive director. She helped organize the People – Pet Partnership in Washington, which gave birth to the Prison Partnership at Purdy.

Delta relies on private donations and membership dues. Membership is open to any interested person. To receive information on the Delta Society or on the human–animal bond programs, write to The Delta Society, P.O. Box 1080, Renton, Washington 98057. The phone number is 206–226–7357.

THE LATHAM FOUNDATION

The Latham Foundation is another nonprofit organization that publishes *The Latham Letter* on the human–animal bond. Headed by president Hugh H. Tebault, Latham works to acquire and to communicate information on how animals help rehabilitate the mentally and physically handicapped and how animals enrich the lives of the elderly.

A major part of Latham's public service is the distribution of documentary films on subjects ranging from basic pet care responsibility for children to animal therapy programs for the disabled. Films for use in education are available, for example, half-hour films on Canine Companions for Independence and the PACT Program, mentioned earlier.

For information write to The Latham Foundation, Latham Plaza Building, Clement and Schiller, Alameda, California 94501. The phone number is 415–521–0920.

APPENDIX B

Service Animals
For The Disabled

SERVICE DOGS FOR THE BLIND

Guide Dogs for the Blind, Inc.
P.O. Box 1200
San Rafael, CA 94915 415–479–4000

Guide Dogs of the Desert
P.O. Box 1692
Palm Springs, CA 92262 714–329–8998

International Guiding Eyes, Inc.
13445 Glenoaks Blvd.
Sylmar, CA 91342 213–362–5834

Fidelco Guide Dogs
P.O. Box 142
Bloomfield, CT 06002 302–243–5200

Eye of the Pacific and Mobility Services, Inc.
2723 Woodlawn Dr.
Honolulu, HI 96822 808–988–6681

Leader Dogs for the Blind
1039 Rochester Rd.
Rochester, MI 48063 313–651–9011

The Seeing Eye, Inc.
P.O. Box 375
Morristown, NJ 07960 201–539–4425

Guide Dog Foundation for the Blind, Inc.
371 E. Jericho Turnpike
Smithtown, NY 11787 212–263–4885

Guiding Eyes for the Blind, Inc.
106 E. 41st St.
New York, NY 10016

Pilot Dogs, Inc.
625 W. Town St.
Columbus OH 43215 614–221–6367

California Eye Dogs Foundation for the Blind
257 S. Spring St.
Los Angeles, CA 90012

SERVICE DOGS FOR THE DEAF

American Humane Association Hearing Dog Program
9725 E. Hampden Ave.
Denver, CO 80231 303–695–0811

Dogs for the Deaf
13260 Highway 238
Jacksonville, OR 97530 503–899–7177

Audio Canes, Inc., Training School
Box 1185
Berkley, MI 48072 313–352–0997

Connecticut Hearing Dog Program
Avery C. Pierce
239 Maple Hill Ave.
Newington, CT 06111

E.A.R. Foundation
Baptist Hospital – West Building
200 Church St.
Nashville, TN 37236 615 – 327 – 4870

Ears for the Deaf
Cheryl Crompton
803 Carlton St.
Mishawaka, IN 46544

Ears for the Deaf
P.O. Box 8482
Kentwood, MI 49508 616 – 455 – 2537

Great Lakes Hearing Dog Program
5800 North Lovers Land Rd.
Milwaukee, WI 53225 414 – 463 – 8300 Voice 414 – 463 – 1990 TTY

Hearing Dog, Inc.
5901 East 89th Ave.
Henderson, CO 80640 303 – 287 – 3277

Hearing Dog of Columbus, Inc.
c/o Mary Jane Stickdale
290 North Hamilton
Gahanna, OH 43230 614 – 471 – 7397

Hearing Dogs for the Deaf
6940 48th St.
Coloma, MI 49038 616 – 468 – 6154

Hearing Ear Dog Program
c/o Bryant Hill Farm
76 Bryant Rd.
Jefferson, MA 01522 617 – 829 – 9745

Harken Hearing Dogs
Susan Beal Brown
165 Stein Rd.
Ann Arbor, MI 48105

Hearing Dogs of the South
Barbara Hennessy
998 Sousa Dr.
Largo, FL 33541

Hearing Ear Dog Program
Kathy Foreman
P.O. Box 213
West Boylston, MA 01583

Hearing Ear Dog Program
17 Leonard Terr.
Wayne, NJ 07470-3337

Red Acre Farm Hearing Dog Center
Box 278
109 Red Acre Rd.
Stow, MA 01775 617 – 897 – 5370 Voice 617 – 897 – 8343 TTY

Residential Dogs
2716 Community Park Dr.
Matthews, NC 28103

Riverside SPCA Hearing Dog Program
Karen Detterich
5791 Fremont St.
Riverside, CA 92504

San Diego Dogs for the Deaf
Patricia Sieglen
P.O. Box 33191
San Diego, CA 92103

San Francisco SPCA Hearing Dog Program
2500 16th St.
San Francisco, CA 94103 415 – 621 – 1700 Voice
415 – 621 – 2174TTY

Speech, Hearing, and Learning Center, Inc.
9 – 11 Medical Court, 811 Pendleton St.
Greenville, SC 29601

SERVICE ANIMALS FOR THE BODILY IMPAIRED

Canine Companions for Independence
Bonita Bergin
P.O. Box 446
Santa Rosa, CA 95401   707 – 528 – 0830

> Northwest Regional Training Center
> 1215 Sebastopol Road
> Santa Rosa, CA 95407
>
> Southwest Regional Office
> P.O. Box 8247
> Rancho Santa Fe, CA 92067
>
> Support Dog Center
> 6901 Harrisburg Pike
> Orient, OH 43146
>
> Northeast Regional Office
> P.O. Box 1178
> White Plains, NY 10602-1178

Feeling Heart Foundation
R.F.D. 2, Box 354
Cambridge, MD 21613   303 – 228 – 3689

Handi-Dogs
Alamo Reaves
P.O. Box 12563
Tucson, AZ 85732   602 – 326 – 3412

Independence Dogs, Inc.
258A Rt. 1
Maple Lane
Chaddsford, PA 19317

Support Dogs for the Handicapped
4419 Butler Hill Road
St. Louis, MO 63128   314 – 487 – 2004

Therapy Dogs, Intl.
1536 Morris Pl.
Hillside, NJ 07205 201 – 968 – 0086

Helping Hands: Simian Aides for the Disabled
(Capuchin monkeys trained to help quadriplegics)
1505 Commonwealth Ave.
Boston, MA 02135 617 – 787 – 4419

Dr. Ruckert and her Rottweiler co-therapist Delilah (Panamint Tipp V. Odenwald, CD)

Janet Ruckert has been a psychotherapist for children and adults for twenty years. She is a doctor of educational psychology and the former president of the Gestalt Therapy Institute of Los Angeles. She has taught creative expression and Gestalt therapy at U.C.L.A. Dr. Ruckert is a member of the California Psychological Association, the American Psychological Association, and the Delta Society, an international group of scientists, educators, and doctors devoted to the understanding of relationships between people and animals.